# NOW THAT I'M...

# CALIFORNIA NOTARY PUBLIC...

# WHAT THE "HECK" DO I DO?

***A PRACTICAL "HANDS ON" GUIDE FOR***

***THE CALIFORNIA NOTARY PUBLIC AND***

***THE CALIFORNIA LOAN SIGNING SPECIALIST***

**Stephanie L. Hulme, N.P., CNI**
**Susan M. Allen**
**© 2004 - 2013**
**(2013 Edition)**

# *INTRODUCTION*

As Notary Instructors, a very common question we are asked is ..."HOW DO I PERFORM MY NOTARIAL DUTIES...and feel confident that I am following the California State Laws?"

You may be a recently commissioned notary, or an experienced notary. This handbook will be beneficial to you regardless of your experience. We will give you step by step illustration and instruction on a number of notarial processes and "real world" examples. Our objective is for you to feel confident when you are doing your notarial process.

We have heard so many stories from notaries stating they've had their commission for ***months*** and haven't done a thing with it! Notaries Public are constantly saying "I haven't done a notary yet. I'm scared about the process". "How do I know if I'm filling out my sequential journal correctly"? We hear this time and time again...

We, the authors, Stephanie Hulme, and Susan M. Allen, have over fifteen years combined experience in the notary profession! For this reason, we decided to write this practical "hands on" guide to facilitate the process for you. You will be able to carry this handbook with you to answer questions and deal with situations that arise in the field. In many instances, this handbook will be a reference guide to help you decide what to do in your particular case. We've even included blank pages (98-101 for you to write notes, and reminders you may need for future reference. And remember, you can write notes on ALL pages if you need to...after all, this is YOUR book!

We have a special section relating to the "Loan Signing" process. We believe this will be a great reference tool.

As you are reviewing this guide, and you have Notary Law questions, please refer to your current California State Notary Public Handbook.

In some cases we have referenced the specific code that applies. It will be designated by the code number in parenthesis, illustrated as follows:

*(California State Code / Gov. Code Section #8207)*

When you see this, please reference the current California State Notary Public Hand Book. If you don't have a current California State Notary Public Handbook, please contact the Secretary of State at 916.653.3595. As a California Notary Public you must be aware that there could be changes in laws and procedures every year, and you must be aware of them. You may contact the California Secretary of State – Notary Section for updates. *We maintain the integrity of our handbook and update it every year.*

(Disclaimer: NOW THAT I'M A CALIFORNIA NOTARY PUBLIC...WHAT THE "HECK" DO I DO? Handbook is not intended to supercede any California State Notary Codes and Regulations. If you have any specific questions relating to the notary codes, please contact the Secretary State of California – Notary section).

**COPYRIGHT © 2004 - 2011 ALL RIGHTS RESERVED. No part of this Handbook may be reproduced or transmitted in any form, in whole or in part, by any means. This includes electronic, mechanical, photocopy, and recording, or by any information storage or retrieval system without prior written consent of both the authors, Stephanie Hulme and Susan M. Allen. (060611)**

*THIS PAGE LEFT BLANK INTENTIONALLY*

# *TABLE OF CONTENTS*

# TABLE OF CONTENTS

# TABLE OF CONTENTS

*THIS PAGE LEFT BLANK INTENTIONALLY*

## *BASIC SUPPLIES YOU WILL NEED*
### *(IN AN OFFICE ENVIRONMENT AND AS A MOBILE NOTARY)*

- Sequential Journal
- Notary Seal
- Embosser (not required in California)
- Inkless thumb printer
- Kleenex or hand wipes (for thumb printer)
- Blank 10 x 13 and legal size manila envelopes
- Notary receipt book
- Loose leaf certificates-
  *Acknowledgment Certificates Jurat*
  *Certificates Subscribing Witness*
  *Acknowledgment Power of Attorney*
  *Certification Sequential Journal*
  *Certification Copy Certification by*
  *Document Holder*
- Black and blue ink pens
- Post-it tabs and "Sign Here" tabs
- One fine point sharpie (medical situations)
- Stapler (standard size staples) & remover
- Ruler (to assist you in making straight lines on your forms as needed).
- Current year "California State Notary Public Hand Book

## *BASIC SUPPLIES YOU WILL NEED AS A MOBILE NOTARY*

- A Vehicle!
- Legal forms (for purchase by the principal).
  *Power of Attorney forms Limited*
  *Power of Attorney forms Health*
  *Care Directives Quitclaim*
  *Deeds*
- Rescission Calendar for the current year.
- Map Book
- AND...all of the Basic Supplies listed above.

*THIS PAGE LEFT BLANK INTENTIONALLY*

## *SAFETY CONCERNS FOR THE MOBILE NOTARY*

*"BETTER SAFE THAN SORRY"*

Try and schedule day appointments.

If you go out at night, tell someone where you're going and when you're expected back.

Carry a charged cell phone.

Carry a map book and stay on busy main streets. If you're unfamiliar with an area, take someone with you.

Listen to your instincts. If something causes you concern, there's nothing wrong with rescheduling your appointment for another time or a public place.

If a signer becomes angry or threatening and asks you to do an improper notarization, do not argue with them or provoke them. Tell them you are sorry and cannot finish the notarization and leave. Record it in your journal.

Make sure your vehicle is in good repair and has plenty of gas.

## *THE NOTARY SEAL*

The Notary Seal is required for all documents you will notarize. Your seal must be in good working order at all times. Always keep an extra ink cartridge or refill ink cartridge available. Do "Test" stamping as needed. Placement of your seal should be as close to your notary signature as possible, within the notarial instruction area. Your seal must be legible and may not touch any printed matter.

***(California State Code / Gov. Code Section #8207)***

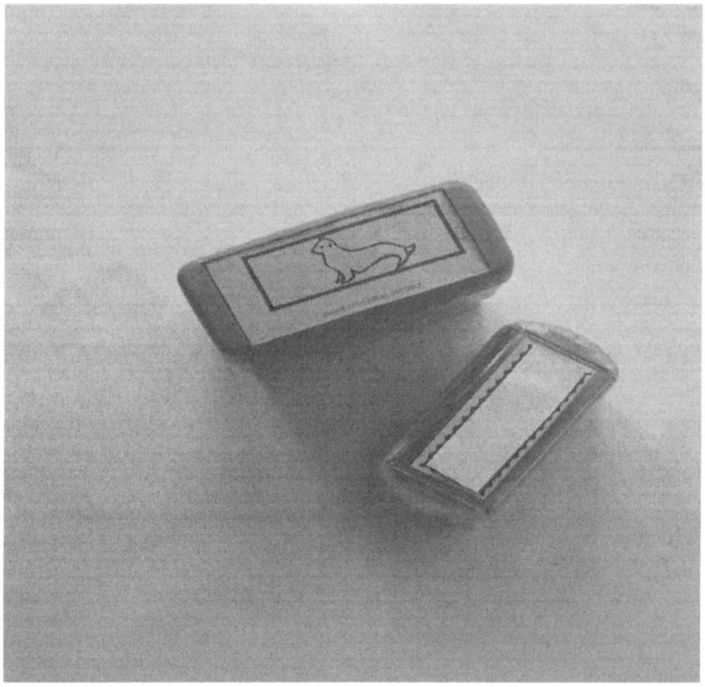

# *THE NOTARY EMBOSSER*

In California the Embosser Seal is ***not required***, although it can be used in conjunction with the Notary Seal.

The embosser reduces the possibility of fraud.

For example, if you are notarizing a 6 page document and you emboss each page, (assuming there is room – without touching any printed matter on the front or back of the document), it would be impossible to insert a "changed" or "extra" page to the document. Any sheet that was added later would not have the embossed area on that particular document. Therefore it would prove that it was not part of the original notarization.

***(California State Code / Gov. Code Section #8207)***

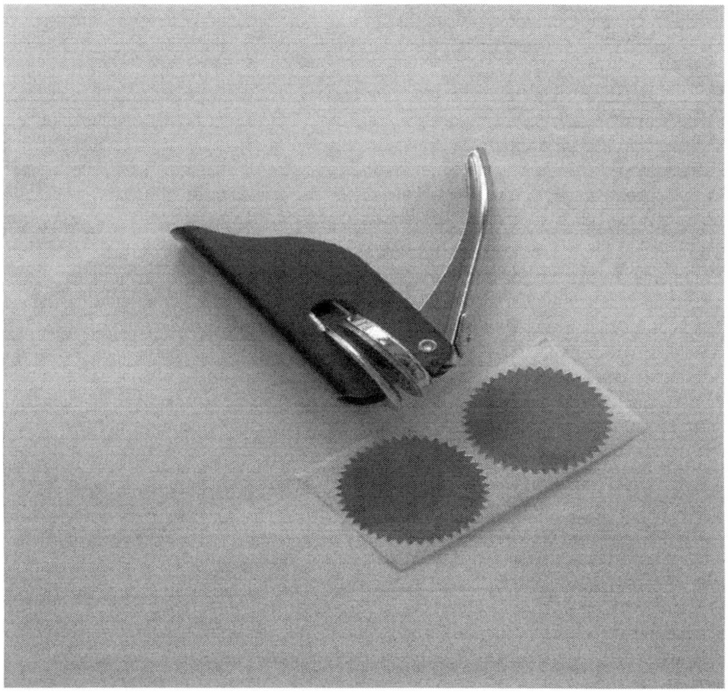

*THIS PAGE LEFT BLANK INTENTIONALLY*

## *THE SEQUENTIAL JOURNAL*

We will review in detail how to fill out your Sequential Journal.

As you know, the Sequential Journal is considered a one "line item entry" even though it consists of 2 pages -from left to right, in your Sequential Journal.

You, as the Notary Public, are the keeper of this Journal for the State of California. It is ***not*** public domain.

If you are working for a private employer (not state, county or school district) who paid for you to go to a Notary School to prepare you for your test, paid for all your supplies, and even allows you to do Notary Services "on the side" during business hours…does he get special privileges because of this? Absolutely not!

If you are fired or you terminate your employment, do you have to surrender your Sequential Journal at that time? Absolutely not!

***(California State Code / Gov. Code Section #8206)***

## *SEQUENTIAL JOURNAL ENTRIES*

| DATE / TIME OF NOTARIZATION | TYPE OF SERVICE | DOCUMENT DATE | TYPE OR TITLE OF DOCUMENT | NAME / ADDRESS OF SIGNER |
|---|---|---|---|---|
| June 15, 2004<br><br>3:45 P.M.<br><br>1 | Jurat<br><br>2 | June 12, 2004<br><br>3 | Short Form<br>Deed of Trust<br>Pages: 2<br>Printed-1 side<br><br>4 | Jane M. Doe<br>1234 Happy Trail Lane<br>Happy Trail, CA 12345-6789<br>PH: 123/456/7890<br><br>5 |

1

In this column you will input the actual date and time of the notarization. Don't forget to indicate A.M. or P.M. next to the time. Please reference the above example.

2

In this column write the type of service you are performing. In this specific case we performed a Jurat service.

3

In this column you write the date the document was created. If there is no document date, then you may write "no document date".

4

In this column you will indicate the type or title of the document. Please see the example above; we have indicated that the type of document was a "Short Form Deed of Trust". Although it is not State Code, you may also indicate how many pages your document is, and if the document(s) is/ are printed on both sides.

5

In this column you will write the complete name and address of the principal that is on their identification they are using. It is always better to have more information than not enough – it is recommended that you also request the principal's area code and phone number.

## *SEQUENTIAL JOURNAL ENTRIES*

| SIGNER ID TYPE OF ID USED | ADDITIONAL INFORMATION | FEE FOR NOTARY SERVICE | SIGNATURE | THUMBPRINT |
|---|---|---|---|---|
| 6 | 7 | 8 | 9 | 10 |

### 6

In this column you will input the source you used to ID the person that presented the document for notarization. For example, if you used Satisfactory Evidence with the use of their California Driver's License you would input the information in the column as per the above example. In this column you would also indicate if the person for that line item is a Credible Witness, Subscribing Witness, or if the person was Personally Known to the Principal or the Notary.

### 7

In this column you will write any additional information that may be required by the State of California Codes, or any other pertinent information that you feel is important to the Notary Service. It is in this area you would indicate if you gave the Principal an Oath or Affirmation. (See Oath or Affirmation).

### 8

In this column you will indicate the fee that you charged for the specified type of notarial service. Remember, you cannot charge more than the specified amount determined by the California Secretary of State.

### 9

In this column you will have the person whose signature you are notarizing sign your Sequential Journal.

### 10

In this column you will have the person who signed your Sequential Journal apply his/her right thumbprint, if required. In the event that the right thumbprint is not available, you may use the left thumb print. You must specify if you did not use the right thumb.

## *STEPS A NOTARY PUBLIC MUST ALWAYS FOLLOW*

- Principal(s) must appear in person except when using a Subscribing Witness, or an Attorney in Fact.
- Identify the Principal through satisfactory evidence or personal knowledge.
- Determine competence and willingness of the principal by asking questions. If you are unsure, ask questions pertaining to that particular document in all situations.
- Look for incomplete documents.
- Fill out the Sequential Journal and have the principal sign his/her name in your journal, and thumb print if required.
- Fill out Acknowledgment or Jurat – give oath or affirmation if required.
- If you are not sure the wording of an out of state Acknowledgment or Jurat follows our California State Code, you may attach a loose leaf certificate.
- Affix your signature and seal properly.
- If you make a mistake – line through the error, initial and date.
- Under any and all circumstances...**DO NOT GIVE LEGAL ADVICE**!

## *CONCERNS OF THE NEW NOTARY...*

- It is important to remember that the majority of your notarial work will be an Acknowledgment or Jurat service.

- The name of the document or type of document may be different in every case, but the type of notary instruction will either be an Acknowledgment or Jurat – that does not change.

- Don't be intimidated if they present a document you are not familiar with – IT DOES NOT MATTER! Remember, the service you will provide will be an Acknowledgment or Jurat.

- If you use a loose leaf certificate the same is true. The loose leaf certificate will either be an Acknowledgment or Jurat.
  The most important thing is that you feel comfortable in the process.

- Conflict of interest – if you have financial or beneficial interest in a document you may not notarize it.

  ***(California State Code / Gov. Code Section #8224)***

- If a company (or principal), should ask you to fill out a Loose Leaf Certificate that is not attached to a document...DON'T DO IT! Remember...Loose Leaf Certificates (Acknowledgments or Jurats) need to be attached to the document at the time of notarization!

- When requesting the identification from a principal and they hand you a "temporary renewal" document from the Department of Motor Vehicles (even though it may have all the information you need, including a photo of the principal), you CANNOT use the temporary renewal as identification. You need the actual permanent plastic card issued by the Department of Motor Vehicles.

## *AS A NOTARY PUBLIC YOU WILL ABSOLUTELY NEVER...*

- **Absolutely Never** read a document! You may scan the document for completeness and the title of the document.
- **Absolutely Never** mark or highlight the document to indicate where the borrower needs to sign or initial the document. If time allows, the best process is to use "sign here" stickers or "post it notes" for reference. (For loan document signing, this is a great help, (if time permits).
- **Absolutely Never** forget to verify a principle's identification. This is, of course, required by the State of California Code.
- **Absolutely Never** accept an expired identification.
- **Absolutely Never** notarize an incomplete document! Always ask if the document is complete.
- **Absolutely Never** **GIVE LEGAL ADVICE** in any practice, process, or procedure.
- **Absolutely Never** change documents you are notarizing. (Unless it is within the notarial instructions)
- **Absolutely Never** back date or postdate a notarized signature.
- **Absolutely Never** use an interpreter...you can't understand what they are saying to the principal...the principal only knows what the interpreter is saying.
- **Absolutely Never** rush through the notary process, under any circumstances. As a notary you must question why someone would say to you..."Can we hurry up this process"? Take as much time as you need - at all times!
- **Absolutely Never** forget to verify your work prior to the completion of the notarial process. Did you get your thumbprint, signature, ID number, etc. We know it sounds crazy, but errors can occur - double check your work!

## *AS A NOTARY PUBLIC YOU WILL **ABSOLUTELY NEVER**...*

- **Absolutely Never** fail to be meticulous in all your Journal Entries! A good guideline to follow is be sure you can explain or defend any entry you have made in your Sequential Journal. Document everything that took place during that particular notary.
- **Absolutely Never** do a Jurat instruction for a Subscribing Witness or an Attorney in fact. A Subscribing Witness and an Attorney in fact are actually signing for the principal, who is NOT there to be placed under oath or affirmation.
- **Absolutely Never** touch anything that belongs to the principal. You will ask the principal to remove their identification from their wallet. You can touch the documents. That is it! Don't set yourself up for a lawsuit. When the process is complete, hand the identification source back to the principal.
- **Absolutely Never** forget that you are a Sworn Officer of the State and you must know your California Codes. Follow these codes at all times. Never do anything unbecoming to the Notary Public profession.
- **Absolutely Never** forget that you cannot use pencil to process your signings. Only blue or black ink!
- **Absolutely Never** keep your Sequential Journal if you decide to resign your commission, or let your commission expire. Turn in your completed Sequential Journals to the County Clerk's office where you took your oath, and filed your bond. If your Sequential Journal is not complete, but you decide not to renew your commission, you must turn in your Sequential Journal to the County Clerk's office where you took your oath, and filed your bond.
- **Absolutely Never** forget to collect all of your supplies (especially your Commission Stamp, Embosser and Sequential Journal) after your notarization is complete...

## *CIRCUMSTANCES YOU SHOULD BE AWARE OF*

- If an ID card is presented by the principal that reads "John Doe Smith" the notary may accept any of the following names for the wording on the Acknowledgment.

  John Smith, John D. Smith, or J. Smith

  The notary may not put in the Acknowledgment wording more than what appears on the ID. For example: You may not write "John Doe Smith" if his ID only says "John D. Smith".

- A principal presents to you ( the notary) a document that has an Acknowledgment instruction on it. You check her ID and the last name is different. She informs you she recently got married and hasn't changed her drivers' license.

  You may be able to use an "AKA" or "Also Known As" procedure. With an AKA signature, the principal would sign her name as it appears on her ID, write "AKA" or "Also Known As" and then sign her name as it appears on the document. The notary can then notarize the name that appears on the ID and this is the only name that will be written on the Acknowledgment certificate.

  It is a good idea for the principal to check with the company receiving the document to make sure an AKA signature will be accepted. Some title companies, banks, and escrow companies will not accept AKA signatures per their company policy. Remember only use the name on the ID in the Acknowledgment certificate. This is the only name for the principal that provides satisfactory evidence of identification - for you as a notary.

- Don't make copies of documents and keep them. The principal(s) documents are a very private and personal matter. Keeping a detailed and accurate Sequential Journal is all that's necessary.

## *CIRCUMSTANCES YOU SHOULD BE AWARE OF*

***Continued***

- If the document has no notarial instructions you may ask the principal(s) what type of notary instruction do you want used for the document? If they cannot tell you what instruction needs to be used, (either Acknowledgment or Jurat) then suggest they contact the document creator. If the document creator is not available, then as a notary, you can ask them what instructions they want you to use. Explain the difference of the Acknowledgment and Jurat. Let them know that if you use an Acknowledgment "I will need to identify you through your ID, you must personally appear, and acknowledge signing the document". For a Jurat, "I also need an ID, and I will put you under oath or affirmation -you must sign the document in my presence". With this information the principal(s) will be able to determine what type of service you will use. As a Notary Public, you *CANNOT* decide for them. NO EXCEPTIONS!

- If you have an Acknowledgment from another state – and it's to be recorded in California, you must attach a California Loose Leaf Certificate, so it follows California State wording. Below the notarial instructions that you are not going to use, write "See attached Acknowledgment Certificate", also initial and date. Attach the Loose Leaf Acknowledgment to the back of the page. You do not have to line through the instructions on the page that you did not use. When they see the attached Acknowledgment, they will know what you did.

- If someone calls you after a notarization and tells you that you made a mistake in the notary instructions: You and you alone must correct the Acknowledgment or Jurat. Anyone else's handwriting on the instructions will raise suspicions of tampering with the document. If it needs to be corrected **you** must correct it. If it's a major mistake, re-notarize the document with the date you are returning, and have the principal(s) personally appear.

- If you have a partially-sighted or blind principal, you the notary, must make sure the signer knows exactly what he/she is signing. Ask him to verify the type or title of the document and its intended effect. If you're uncertain, ask an impartial person to read the document to him before you proceed.

- If you have a document with NCR (no carbon required) paper, ask the principal, "Do you want each sheet (original and copy) notarized or just the original?" If the principal says notarize original and each copy, you make a separate entry in your Sequential Journal for the copy(s). Treat the copy as the original and have him sign the copy(s) also (even if it went through the carbon, it needs to be an original signature not a copy of one). You may charge for the copy also, because you're treating it as an original. In most cases, the principal will not want the copy notarized, because it's just for their record.

- When you look at a document to put the information in your Sequential Journal, check the notary instructions and see if there's enough room for the seal. If there is not enough room next to your signature, you can fit your rectangular seal "on end" to fit in the margin, next to the notary instructions. If there is not enough room, you will have to attach a loose leaf certificate. Write on the bottom of the document "see attached loose leaf certificate", initial, and date.

- A lot of people come to a notary to have a photograph notarized. Regardless of the reason for the request, you'll have to respond, "Sorry, I'm not able to do that!" The reason a notary cannot notarize a photograph is because a written statement and a signature, must appear on paper before it can be categorized as a document.

  *There is a solution, in some circumstances.* If a principal chooses to write and sign a document attached to the back of the photograph saying, for example; "The photograph attached to this document is of me, Betty Fine ," the notary can notarize the signature if all the procedures follow California State Code. A certificate is signed, and sealed. What type of service will you perform in this case? Remember, you cannot give legal advice. What will you do? As a Notary Public you can explain the type of service you can perform...Acknowledgment or Jurat. Once you have explained the difference, the principal(s) must tell you what type of notarization to do.

# *COPY CERTIFICATION BY DOCUMENT HOLDER*

- If someone comes to you to certify a copy of a driver's license, passport, apply for pension, provide proof of residency, or other documents of this nature, you may not certify it under California State Code. However, you may use what is called a "Copy Certification by Document Custodian" (see below for wording).

***Remember...***
***This process is not for vital records or documents to be recorded.***

This process is an alternative to the notary "certified copy", which can only be either 1) a one line item entry of your Sequential Journal or 2) a Power of Attorney. The custodian of the original document writes a statement certifying that a photocopy of the original is true and correct. The notary executes a Jurat below the custodian's name.

## Sample:

State of California County of_____________

I, ____________, hereby declare that the attached reproduction of
Name of Custodian of Original Document

______________________________
Description of Original Document

is a true, correct, and complete photocopy of a document in my possession or control.

______________________________
Signature of Custodian of Original Document

______________________________
Address

(Seal)

______________________________

Subscribed and sworn to (or affirmed) before me this_______ day of________________,20______.
Day Month Year
Proved to me on the basis of satisfactory evidence to be the person(s) who appeared before me.

______________________________
Signature of Notary Public

# *NOTARY FEES*

## MAXIMUM FEES A NOTARY CAN CHARGE A CLIENT

- ACKNOWLEDGMENT PER SIGNATURE $10.00
- JURAT (INCLUDES OATH) $10.00
- CERTIFYING POWER OF ATTORNEY $10.00

**(FOR OTHER FEE REQUIREMENTS SEE THE CURRENT CALIFORNIA STATE CODE BOOK)**

***(California State Code / Gov. Code Section #8211)***

**i.e.:** If you have 4 signatures on 1 document that need to be notarized, you can charge $10.00 per signature = $40.00 total charge.

How many journal entries will you have to record in your Sequential Journal? You guessed right! 4 entries.

# *TRAVEL FEES*

- Consider the number of miles you will travel.
- Consider the travel time required.
- Consider the time of day – If it is a week day, evening, weekend, or holiday.
- Consider the time of the appointment…is it an emergency or after 8:00 P.M.?
- Consider "repeat business" as a reason to waive the travel fees, or at least reduce them. This would also depend on how many miles you will be traveling from your home base. Remember, we are not in business to lose money!
- Do not price yourself out of the market. If you do, your next question will be "why isn't anyone calling me?"

# *OATHS AND AFFIRMATIONS*

An Oath is a spoken pledge by a person who solemnly promises truthfulness in completing an act. In an Oath there is reference to a Supreme Being, i.e.: “So help you God”.

An Affirmation may be taken by a person who objects to taking an Oath due to the reference of a Supreme Being.

The following are examples of **Oaths**:

- “Do you solemnly state that the statements in this document are true, so help you God?”
- “Do you solemnly state that the statements in this document are true and correct for all intents and purposes, so help you God?”
- “Do you solemnly state to tell the truth, the whole truth, and nothing but the truth, so help you God?”

The following are examples of **Affirmations**:

- “Do you solemnly state, under penalty of perjury that the statements in this document are true?”
- “Do you solemnly state, under penalty of perjury that the statements in this document are true and correct for all intents and purposes?”
- “Do you solemnly state, under penalty of perjury to tell the truth, the whole truth, and nothing but the truth?”

## ***THUMBPRINT***

A thumbprint is ***required*** if the document to be notarized is a…

- ***DEED***
- ***DEED OF TRUST QUITCLAIM DEED***
- ***POWER OF ATTORNEY***
- ***DOCUMENT AFFECTING REAL PROPERTY***

Although it is ***not required***, some Notaries will request a thumbprint in every process. If you request a thumbprint, and it is not required, the principal(s) may refuse. If that is the case and all California Code criteria are met, you must do the notary process.

When taking a thumbprint, have them ink the right thumb and place it flat in designated box. Place the right thumb straight down and lift straight up. Instruct them not to "roll" the thumb

***(California State Code / Gov. Code Section #8206, #2-G)***

# *INCOMPLETE DOCUMENT*

- You MAY NOT notarize a document that is incomplete.
- Scan the document for blank spaces.
- If there are blank spaces, ask the principal if the spaces need to be filled in. If so, they must be filled in prior to notarization.
- If the principal says the document is incomplete and cannot be filled in at that time, you MAY NOT notarize the document.
- If there are blank spaces and the principal says the document is complete, you may notarize the document. Note in your Sequential Journal that the "signer stated document is complete".
- If pages are numbered, be sure to count each page and verify all pages are there. If they are not there, tell the principal you need the complete document, before you can notarize the document.
- A document that is to be recorded contains blank spaces for the County Recorder to fill out (typically located in the upper left hand corner of the document). If these are the only blank spaces – separate from the body of the document – it is complete. You may notarize the document.
- Regarding notarization of Deeds, Short Form Deeds of Trust, Quitclaim Deeds, or any deeds that describe real property, YOU MUST BE AWARE that within the area of the description of the property you may see the words "Schedule A" or "Exhibit A". If that is the case be sure to locate the document "Schedule A" or "Exhibit A". It must be with the paperwork you are notarizing. If "Schedule A" or "Exhibit A" cannot be located, you may not notarize the document because it is an "incomplete document".

***(California State Code / Gov. Code Section #8205)***

## *PERSONAL KNOWLEDGE AND SATISFACTORY EVIDENCE*

- Personal Knowledge – Having familiarity with an individual resulting from personal interactions over a given period of time. Not casual acquaintance, also must produce one of the following I.D.'s.

- Satisfactory Evidence – all "CURRENT" ID's include: DMV California Identification Card DMV California Drivers License All states DMV ID and Drivers License Canadian or Mexican Drivers License Armed Forces ID Inmate ID card – only if in custody

  DMV California Identification card

  DMV California Drivers License

  All States DMV ID and Drivers License

  Canadian or Mexican Drivers License

  Military/Armed Forces ID Card

  Inmate ID card – *only* if in custody

  United States Passport

  Foreign Passport stamped with U.S. Visa

  ID card issued by an agency or office of the State of California or by an agency or office of a City or County of California.

# *CREDIBLE WITNESS*

Remember a Credible Witness is a "walking, talking, ID card".

When a principal appears before a notary and does not have the ID required by law, the principal may be identified by one Credible Witness who is personally known to the notary and provide a required I.D.

A Credible Witness appears in person to verify the identity of the principal who appears before the notary.

The notary will put the Credible Witness under oath or affirmation with the following questions.

**<u>Oath or Affirmation for 1 Credible Witnesses:</u>**
**Do you personally know the principal?**
**Answer: Must be Yes**
**Do you have any beneficial or financial interest or named in the document?**
**Answer: Must be No**
**Do you know the principal does not have an ID and it is difficult for him to get one?**
**Answer: Must be Yes**
**Is the principal the same person named in the document?**
**Answer: Must be Yes**

You will fill out a one line item entry in your Sequential Journal and have them sign the journal. You do not charge a fee for a Credible Witness.

Remember:

- *A Credible Witness must be personally known to the notary and produce a required I.D.*
- *A Credible Witness must not have any beneficial or financial Interest, or be named in the document.*
- *A Credible Witness knows the principal has no ID, and finds it difficult to get a new one.*
- *A Credible Witness knows the principal's name is the same one on the document.*

***(California State Code / Gov. Code Section #8206 - Civil Code #1185)***

# *TWO CREDIBLE WITNESSES*

When a principal appears before a notary and does not have the ID required by law, the principal may be identified by two Credible Witnesses. They do not have to know the notary.

Two Credible Witnesses <u>must be</u> personally known to the principal. They will appear in person with their current valid ID to verify the identity of the principal who appears before the notary. The notary will put the Credible Witnesses under oath or affirmation with the following questions.

**<u>Oath or Affirmation for 2 Credible Witnesses:</u>**
**Do you personally know the principal?**
**Answer: Must be Yes**
**Do you have any beneficial or financial interest or named in the document?**
**Answer: Must be No**
**Do you know the principal does not have an ID and it is difficult for him to get one?**
**Answer: Must be Yes**
**Is the principal the same person named in the document?**
**Answer: Must be Yes**

You will fill out a one line item entry in your Sequential Journal for each Credible Witness, and each witness must sign the journal on their own designated line. You <u>do not</u> charge a fee for Credible Witnesses.

Remember:

- *A Credible Witness must be personally known to the notary.*
- *A Credible Witness must not have any beneficial or financial Interest, or be named in the document.*
- *A Credible Witness knows the principal has no ID, and finds it difficult to get a new one.*
- *A Credible Witness knows the principal's name is the same one on the document.*

***(California State Code / Gov. Code Section #8206 - Civil Code #1185)***

# ***ACKNOWLEDGMENT***

- The Acknowledgment instruction for the most part is printed at the end of the document.

- The Principal(s) must appear in person.

- You must personally know the principal(s) and they must provide a required I.D. or ID them through Satisfactory Evidence. (see Personal Knowledge and Satisfactory Evidence page in this guide).

- Fill out your Sequential Journal.

- Have the principal sign your journal and thumb print if required.

- Principal(s) signs the document of his/her own free will.

- If the document has been signed, the principal must verbally acknowledge signing the document.

- Fill out Acknowledgment instructions – or if required – a loose leaf Acknowledgment certificate.

- Remember…the document creator or principal(s) must decide the type of notary instruction you are to use - a Jurat or Acknowledgment, if there are no instructions!

- California State Code requires you to use the Acknowledgment (see page 26) set forth in the statute rather than the variations we sometimes see. If the document is from another state this does not apply – unless it is to be recorded in California.

  Please see the following page for instruction on how to fill out the Acknowledgment Certificate.

  ***(California State Code / Civil Code Section #1189)***

# *ACKNOWLEDGMENT CERTIFICATE*

STATE OF ______**1**________
COUNTY OF______**2**________

On_______**3**______ before me, ( (4) here insert name and title of the officer), personally appeared

_________________________5_______________________________

Proved to me on the basis of satisfactory evidence to be the person(s) whose name(s) is/are subscribed to the within instrument and acknowledge to me that he/she/they executed the **6** same in his/her/their authorized capacity(ies), and that by his/her/their signature(s) on the instrument the person(s), or the entity upon behalf of which the person(s) acted, executed the instrument. I certify under PENALTY OF PERJURY under the laws of the state of California that the foregoing paragraph is true and correct.

WITNESS my hand and official seal.

**8**
(SEAL)

_____________**7**_____________
SIGNATURE OF NOTARY

**9**
(EMBOSSER)

Note: The embosser is not required by California Notary Law.

## ***HOW TO FILL OUT THE ACKNOWLEDGMENT***

Remember to fill out the Acknowledgment as we have illustrated to the left of this page. Remember, if the wording is not complete, you must fill out and attach a California Acknowledgment Loose Leaf Certificate.

1 ***STATE OF***: Must be in the State of California

2 ***COUNTY OF***: Input the County you are in at the time of the notarization.

3 ***ON***: Date of the notarization.

4 ***BEFORE ME***: Print your name as it appears on your commission. You must put, "Notary Public" after your commission name on the acknowledgment.

5 ***PERSONALLY APPEARED***: Principal(s) name(s) as it appears on the document signature line.

6 ***CROSS OUT WITH ONE STRAIGHT LINE:*** Anything that does not apply. Person(s), is/are, he/she/they and his/hers/their. Remember, not filling out this section of the notarial instruction will cause the notarization to be incorrect. It could lead to fines and a potential law suit.

7 ***SIGNATURE OF NOTARY***: Sign your name as it appears on your commission.

8 ***SEAL***: Will be stamped on the left side of your signature or as close to your signature as possible.

9 ***EMBOSSER***: If you choose to use one you can emboss as close to your seal as you can without embossing printed matter.

Note: On occasion documents require your commission expiration date, if so, you may include it in the box provided.

***THIS PAGE LEFT BLANK INTENTIONALLY***

# *JURAT*

- The Jurat instructions are usually printed at the end of the document.
- The principal(s) must appear in person.
- ID is required as of January 1, 2005. – If you personally know the principal(s) they must provide the required I.D. or identify them through Satisfactory Evidence. (see Personal Knowledge and Satisfactory Evidence page in this guide book.
- Fill out your Sequential Journal with the necessary information and have the Principal(s) sign in the appropriate area.
- Place the Principal(s) under oath or affirmation. (See Oaths or Affirmations in this guide for detail).
- Have the Principal(s) sign the document.
- If the Principal(s) signed the document prior to the notarization appointment, have the principal re-sign the document in your presence.
- Fill out the Jurat instructions – if they are not complete on the document, you may fill out a loose leaf Jurat certificate and staple it to the page you would have notarized.
- The following pages will give you step by step instruction on “How to fill out the Jurat”.
- Remember…the principal must decide whether to use a Jurat or Acknowledgment if there are no instructions!

(California State Code / Civil Code Section #1189)

## *JURAT CERTIFICATE*

**State of ______1_______,**
**County of ______2_____**

**Subscribed and sworn to (or affirmed) before me on this __3__ day of ________, 20___, by ______4_________ Proved to me on the basis of satisfactory evidence to be the person(s) who appeared before me.**

**6 (SEAL)**

**__________5__________**
**SIGNATURE OF NOTARY**

7
(EMBOSSER)

Note: The embosser is not required by California Notary Law.

## ***HOW TO FILL OUT THE JURAT***

Remember to fill out the Jurat as we have illustrated to the left of this page. Remember, if the wording is not complete, you must fill out and attach a California Jurat Loose Leaf Certificate.

1 ***STATE OF*:** Must be in the State of California.

2 ***COUNTY OF***: Input the county you are physically in, at the time of the notarization.

3 ***SUBSCRIBED AND SWORN TO BEFORE ME ON:*** Date of Notarization

4 ***BY:*** Print the Principal(s) name.

5 ***SIGNATURE OF NOTARY:*** Sign your name as it appears on your commission.

6 ***SEAL:*** You will stamp your seal on the left side of your signature or as close to your signature as possible.

7 ***EMBOSSER:*** If you chose to use one, you can emboss as close to the seal or your signature as you can, without embossing printed matter.

# *SIGNATURE BY MARK*

- The Principal is identified through Personal Knowledge, and provide required I.D. or Satisfactory Evidence. This process does not change.
- Two witnesses must be present. They do not need ID and do not have to know the Principal.
- The witnesses will watch the Principal make his/her mark in your Sequential Journal and on the document.
- The first witness will <u>sign the principal's name (in Script)</u> on the document next to his/her mark.
- Both witnesses must sign and print their names on the document near the Principal's mark. Witness number one (that signed the principal's name near his/her mark will sign first. Witness number two will sign below witness number one.
- Fill out your Sequential Journal as usual with the principal's information. The first witness will sign the principal's name next to his mark in the journal.
- In the additional information area of your journal, have both witnesses sign their names. (This is not required, but highly recommended).
- Fill out the Acknowledgment. Input the principal's name in the personally appeared area.
- If you have any questions about how to fill out the Acknowledgment, please review that section.
- If the principal has no ID you can ID him using 2 Credible Witnesses, who may also serve as witnesses for the signature by mark. If you use 2 Credible Witnesses, you must enter a one line item entry in your Sequential Journal for each Credible Witness.

(California State Code / Civil Code Section #14)

## *SIGNATURE BY MARK SALES AGREEMENT*

I, Judy Fine do hereby promise to pay my mother, - Betty Fine of Huntington Beach, California, $8,000.00 that she loaned to me on this date March 3, 2004. The full amount of the loan will be used as the initial down payment for a 2003 Ford Focus.

Dated: June 3, 2004, BY: X 1st witness: Signs principal's name (Mark)
witness: Signs their name

1st witness: Signs their name
2nd witness: Signs their name

STATE OF: California
COUNTY OF: Orange

On June 3, 2004 ,before me, Notary's commission name, (Title) Notary Public personally appeared Judy Fine Proved to me on the basis of satisfactory evidence to be the person(~~s~~) whose name(~~s~~) is/~~are~~ subscribed to the within instrument and acknowledge to me that ~~he~~/she/~~they~~ executed the same in ~~his~~/her/~~their~~ authorized capacity(~~ies~~), and that by ~~his~~/her/~~their~~ signature(~~s~~) on the instrument the person(~~s~~), or the entity upon behalf of which the person(~~s~~) acted, executed the instrument. I certify under PENALTY OF PERJURY under the laws of the state of California that the foregoing paragraph is true and correct.

WITNESS my hand and official seal.

(seal)

Notary's Commission Name
Notary Signature

(EMBOSSER)

Note: The embosser is not required by California Notary Law.

*THIS PAGE LEFT BLANK INTENTIONALLY*

## *POWER OF ATTORNEY CERTIFICATION COPY*

- A Notary Public may certify any original Power of Attorney. You do not have to be the original notary.
- You must photo copy the original Power of Attorney yourself. This insures that it is an exact copy of the original.
- On the following page you will see a Loose Leaf Certificate of the "Certification Copy – Power of Attorney". On page 37 you will be given instruction on how to fill out the certificate.
- Effective January 1, 2008 you are now required to get a thumbprint for power of attorney.

***(California State Code / Probate Code Section #4307)***

## *POWER OF ATTORNEY – CERTIFICATION COPY LOOSE LEAF CERTIFICATE*

State of ________**1**________
County of ________**2**________

I ________**3**________, Notary Public, certify that on ____4______, I examined the original power of attorney and the copy of the power of attorney. I further certify that the copy is a true and correct copy of the original power of attorney.

WITNESS my hand and seal.

**6**
(SEAL)

________**5**________
SIGNATURE OF NOTARY

**7**
(EMBOSSER)

Note: The embosser is not required by California Notary Law.

# *HOW TO FILL OUT THE POWER OF ATTORNEY – CERTIFICATION COPY*

1 ***STATE***: Must be California.

2 ***COUNTY OF***: Input the County you are in at the time of the notarization.

3 ***I*:** Name of Notary Public.

4 ***DATE*:** Date of notarization.

5 ***SIGNATURE OF NOTARY*:** On this line you will sign the name that is on your commission.

6 ***SEAL***: Will be stamped on the left side of your signature.

7 ***EMBOSSER***: If you choose to use one, you can emboss as close to the seal or signature as you can, without embossing printed matter.

## *ATTORNEY IN FACT ACKNOWLEDGMENT*

State of ______1______
County of____2______

On____3______, before me, ____________4_____________ personally appeared ______________5______________ Proved to me on the basis of satisfactory evidence to be the person whose name is subscribed to the within instrument as the attorney in fact of____________6_______________, and acknowledged to me that he/she subscribed the name of ____________7___________thereto as principal and his/her own name as attorney in fact.

WITNESS my hand and seal.

9
(SEAL)

______________8______________
SIGNATURE OF NOTARY

10
(EMBOSSER)

Note: The embosser is not required by California Notary Law.

# *HOW TO FILL OUT ATTORNEY IN FACT ACKNOWLEDGMENT*

1. ***STATE OF***: Must be in State of California

2. ***COUNTY OF***: Input the County you are in at the time of notarization.

3. ***ON***: Date will be the date you are notarizing this document.

4. ***BEFORE ME***: On this line you will write in your commission name.
5. ***PERSONALLY APPEARED***: Name of attorney in fact (person in front of you)

   (Be sure to "strike out" any information that does not apply. i.e.: If female, ~~HE~~/SHE you would strike out ~~HE~~). Remember, not filling out this section of the notarial instruction will cause the notarization to be incorrect. It could lead to fines and a potential law suit.

6. __________________ Principals name

7. __________________ Principals name

8. ***SIGNATURE OF NOTARY***: On this line you will sign the name that is on your commission.

9. ***SEAL***: Will be stamped on the left side of your signature.

10. ***EMBOSSER***: If you choose to use one, you can emboss as close to the seal or signature as you can, without embossing printed matter.

Note:
If you do not have a Loose Leaf "Attorney in Fact Acknowledgment Certificate", don't panic. You may use the Acknowledgment that is on the document or, a California Acknowledgment Loose Leaf Certificate. (The Acknowledgment states "personally appeared" before you, which in this case is the Attorney in Fact).

## *SEQUENTIAL JOURNAL CERTIFICATION COPY LINE-ITEM-ENTRY*

State of ________**1**______
County of ________**2**______

On __________**3**__________, before me, ______________**4**______________________ a Notary Public in and for the State of California, do hereby certify the attached document to be an accurate facsimile of the line item entry number ______**5**______ from page ____**6**____, of the Official Sequential Journal of notarial acts signed by __________**7**__________ acknowledging the original document described or titled as a ________**8**________, notarized on the ____**9**____ day of __________, 20____.

OFFICIAL seal of the Notary Public

**11**
(SEAL)

________________**10**________________
SIGNATURE OF NOTARY

**12**
(EMBOSSER)

Note: The embosser is not required by California Notary Law.

Regarding the above Certification Copy . It is not required by California Notary Law to use a certificate. Per the Office of the Secretary of State, the only requirement is that you enter the information giving a copy of your Sequential Journal Line Item in your Sequential Journal. It is recommended that the individual requesting the copy sign your Sequential Journal.

## *HOW TO FILL OUT THE SEQUENTIAL JOURNAL CERTIFICATION COPY LINE-ITEM-ENTRY*

1. ***STATE***: Must be California.

2. ***COUNTY OF***: Input the county you are in at the time of the notarization.

3. ***ON***: Enter the date you are notarizing the document.

4. ***BEFORE ME***: On this line you will write in your commission name.

5. ***LINE ITEM ENTRY NUMBER***: On this line you will write in the page line item you are copying.

6. ***PAGE NUMBER***: On this line you will write in the page number of the Sequential Journal.

7. ***ACTS SIGNED BY*****:** On this line you will write in the name of the principal acknowledging the original document.

8. ***TITLED AS A*****:** On this line you will write in the name of the document.

9. ***NOTARIZED ON THE*****:** On this line you will write in the date of the original notarization.

10. ***SIGNATURE OF NOTARY*****:** The name that is on your commission.

11. ***SEAL***: Will be stamped on the left side of your signature.

12. ***EMBOSSER***: If you choose to use one, you can emboss as close to the seal or your signature as you can without embossing printed matter.

## *SUBSCRIBING WITNESS / WITH CREDIBLE WITNESS*

A Subscribing Witness is a courier of documents who delivers the documents to the Notary Public, on behalf of the principal. Certain criteria must be followed.

This notarial process is the only type of process where the principal will not be present and standing before the Notary Public.

The Subscribing Witness appears before the notary, who personally knows her/him personally.

The identity of the subscribing witness must be established by the oath of a credible witness who personally knows the subscribing witness and who is known personally by the Notary Public. In addition, the credible witness must present an ID.

The Subscribing Witness must sign the document under the principals' signature. If the document has already been signed, have him/her acknowledge it is their signature. The notary will put the Subscribing Witness under oath or affirmation and ask the following questions:

**Oath or Affirmation for Subscribing Witness:**
**"Do you personally know the principal?"**
**Answer: Must be Yes**
**"Did you see the Principal sign the document or did she acknowledge signing the document?"**
**Answer: Must be Yes and elaborate on the answer..."Yes, I saw the Principal sign the document" or"Yes, the Principal acknowledged signing the document".**
**If the answer is "NO" the Notary will ask the Subscribing Witness...**
**Did the principal acknowledge signing the document?**
**The answer must be Yes "Did the Principal ask you to have the document notarize?"**
**Answer: Must be Yes**

**REMEMBER: THE NOTARY MAY NOT NOTARIZE A DOCUMENT FOR A SUBSCRIBING WITNESS IF IT IS A:**

- ***QUITCLAIM DEED,***
- ***GRANT DEED***
- ***MORTGAGE,***
- ***SECURITY AGREEMENT***
- ***DEED OF TRUST***
- ***POWER OF ATTORNEY***
- ***ANY NOTARY REQUIRING A THUMB PRINT***

**Note: All the above items listed involve Real Property.**

**(California State Code / Civil Code Section #1195)**

## *SUBSCRIBING WITNESS / WITH CREDIBLE WITNESS*

**Continued**

The notary will also give the oath or affirmation to the Credible Witness and ask the following questions:

**<u>Oath or Affirmation for 1 Credible Witnesses:</u>**
**Do you personally know the principal?**
**Answer: Must be Yes**
**Do you have any beneficial or financial interest or named in the document?**
**Answer: Must be No**
**Do you know the principal does not have an ID and is difficult for him to get one?**
**Answer: Must be Yes**
**Is the principal the same person named in the document?**
**Answer: Must be Yes**

Once the Notary Public has verified the answers, and all are answered to the Notary's satisfaction, the Notary will then complete a one line item entry in the Sequential Journal for the Subscribing Witness and also have her/him sign. You will also enter a one line item entry for the Credible Witness and have him/her sign your Sequential Journal. Remember ID is required. The Notary personally knows the Credible Witness, the Credible Witness personally knows the Subscribing Witness and Notary.

In the "Additional Information" box of the Sequential Journal, you will include: The name of the Subscribing Witness and the principal's name and indicate you put them under oath or affirmation and the questions / answers you received.

Remember you will not charge a fee for the Credible Witness only the Subscribing Witness.

## *SUBSCRIBING WITNESS ACKNOWLEDGMENT WITH CREDIBLE WITNESS*

State of California_____1______
County of: ____2_____

On ___3____(date), before me, the undersigned, a Notary Public for the State, personally appeared ___4___(subscribing witness's name), proved to me to be the person whose name is subscribed to the within instrument, as a witness thereto, on the oath of ____5____(credible witness's name), a credible witness who is known to me and provided a satisfactory identifying document. __6___(subscribing witness's name) being by me duly sworn, deposed and said that he/she was present and saw/heard ___7___(name(s) of principal(s)), the same person(s) described in and whose name(s) is/are subscribed to the within, or attached, instrument in his/her/their (8) authorized capacity(ies) as (a) party(ies) thereto, execute or acknowledge executing the same, and that said affiant subscribed his/her name to the within instrument as a witness at the request of ___9__(name(s) of the principal(s)).

WITNESS my hand and seal.

11
(SEAL)

______________10______________
SIGNATURE OF NOTARY

12
(EMBOSSER)

Note: The embosser is not required by California Notary Law.

## *HOW TO FILL OUT A SUBSCRIBING WITNESS WITH CREDIBLE WITNESS LOOSE LEAF ACKNOWLEDGMENT FORM*

1. ***STATE OF***: Must be in State of California
2. ***COUNTY OF***: Input the County you are in at the time of notarization.
3. ***ON***: Date will be the date you are notarizing this document.
4. ***PERSONALLY APPEARED***: The Subscribing Witness name appears there.
5. ____________: Name of Credible Witness.
6. ____________: The subscribing witness's name goes in the blank space.
7. ____________: The principal's name goes in this blank space.
8. ***CROSS OUT WITH ONE STRAIGHT LINE*** Anything that does not apply. Person(s), is/are, he/she/they and his/hers/their. Remember, not filling out this section of the notarial instruction will cause the notarization to be incorrect. It could lead to fines and a potential law suit.
9. ____________: The principal's name goes in this blank space also.
10. ***SIGNATURE OF NOTARY*** : On this line you will sign the name that is on your commission.
11. ***SEAL***: Will be stamped on the left side of your signature.
12. ***EMBOSSER***: If you choose to use one, you can emboss as close to the seal or signature as you can, without embossing printed matter.

*THIS PAGE LEFT BLANK INTENTIONALLY*

## *YOUR FIRST NOTARY ASSIGNMENT*

## *...WILL START WITH A PHONE CALL!*

- Be professional and friendly – smile as you're speaking on the phone. Your clients will sense your attitude.
- Your client requests your notarial services for a notarization.
- Before going further, you should indicate to your client how much you will charge for the services, which should include your travel fees.
- *"I charge $10.00 per signature, plus travel fees*", would be a good response to establish your fee with your client. At this time your client will ask you what your travel fees are. This begins the negotiation of your travel fees.
- Confirm that the signer(s) have the proper ID and all ID(s) are current.
- Once it is established that the principal made a proper request and are able to pay the fees, set your appointment.
- You *must* arrive on time to your appointment

## *INSTRUCTIONS FOR YOUR DAILY NOTARY APPOINTMENTS*

### *Your first call and subsequent calls:*

- **Ask for their name and phone number.**
  What is the document? Does it have notary instructions? Do they have a valid current ID? (This is the time to find out if they will need two Credible Witnesses to identify them). Ask for their address. Set the appointment, and arrive on time.

- **You arrive on time and introduce yourself.**
  Find a suitable working area and set up your supplies - seal, embosser (if you use one), Sequential Journal, pens, thumbprint ink and wet wipes or Kleenex. Open your Sequential Journal, ask the principal(s) for the document(s) and their ID. Scan the document(s) for the date, title, and completeness. Be sure the name on their ID matches the name on the document(s). As stated earlier, if the name on the document does not match the identification, you will need two Credible Witnesses.

- **Fill out your Sequential Journal from left to right.**
  See "How to fill out your Sequential Journal" section of this guide for detailed instructions. Don't forget to have the principal sign your Sequential Journal. If required be sure to get a thumbprint. Set aside your Sequential Journal.

## *INSTRUCTIONS FOR YOUR DAILY NOTARY APPOINTMENTS*

- **Have the principal(s) sign the document as his/her name appears on the document.**

  Fill out the Acknowledgment or Jurat, sign, seal and emboss if you have one. See section for instructions on "How to Fill out Acknowledgment and Jurat" in this guide for detailed instructions.

- D**ouble check**... your Sequential Journal: Be sure that the principal(s) signed your journal and all information is recorded properly. Scan the document(s) to be sure the notary instructions are filled out and you signed and sealed the document(s).

- **Preparing to leave…**
  Return the notarized documents back to the principal(s), along with their ID. Put away all your notarial supplies. Make sure you have ALL your supplies. Leave a business card with your client. Be sure to collect your fees. Thank your client and leave.

***THIS PAGE LEFT BLANK INTENTIONALLY***

# *DOCUMENT SCENARIOS*

The following pages contain 10 scenarios and completed documents (Acknowledgments and Jurats), that you as a Notary Public will face in everyday situations.

The circumstance surrounding the document does not matter. Treat each document the same. Verify that each document is complete.

Please make note that throughout the following scenarios, the notarial instructions are Acknowledgments and Jurats. When it's an Attorney-in-fact or a Subscribing Witness you will always fill out an Acknowledgment for the principal(s) standing in front of you. Some are just worded differently.

If you have an Acknowledgment that you are not sure follows California State Code, attach a loose leaf Acknowledgment or Jurat Certificate and you'll be assured you are following California State Code.

In each of the following scenarios state the fee per signature and the travel fee in the initial phone call with the client. The client must agree to the fees prior to going on the appointment.

Be sure to study the illustrated forms and scenarios to become acquainted with the wording on different documents.

NORTH CAROLINA

FORD COUNTY

IN THE GENERAL COURT OF JUSTICE

DISTRICT COURT DIVISION

File No. 22-891

FRED SNOW )

Plaintiff, )

)

VS.

)

TONY PLOW )

Defendant. )

**AFFIDAVIT OF SERVICE**
**BY REGISTERED OR CERTIFIED MAIL**

I, FRED SNOW (Plaintiff), duly sworn, deposes and says:

Service of process by certified mail, return receipt requested, has been completed on the Defendant, TONY PLOW.

This affidavit is filed pursuant to the requirements of North Carolina Rules of Civil Procedure 4(j2)(2).

1. A copy of the Summons and Complaint was deposited in the Post Office for mailing by certified mail, return receipt requested, and addressed and dispatched to the Defendant.

2. It was mailed to 361 DRIFT LANE, at 361 DRIFT LANE, RAINBOW, NORTH CAROLINA.

3. Service was received on JUNE 4, 2001 by the Defendant as evidenced by the attached green return receipt card and completed pursuant to the requirements of N.C.G.S. 1-75.10(4).

This the 10 th day of JULY, 2001.

Fred Snow
Plaintiff

STATE OF: CALIFORIA
COUNTY OF: ORANGE

SWORN TO AND SUBSCRIBED BEFORE ME

This the 10th day of JULY, 2001, BY FRED SNOW
PROVED TO ME ON THE BASIS OF SATISFACTORY EVIDENCE TO BE THE PERSON(S) WHO APPEARED BEFORE ME.

SIGNED BY NOTARY
Notary Public

My Commission Expires: MAY 7, 2004

# *SCENARIO 1*

## *"AFFIDAVIT OF SERVICE"*

***NORTH CAROLINA FORM***

Fred Snow just moved here from North Carolina. He has an "Affidavit of Service" he would like to have notarized.

You ask him if he has a current valid ID. He has a current driver's license from North Carolina.

Write in the instruction that applies, if their not already printed on the document.

Fill out a one line item in your Sequential Journal, have him sign your book and give him his oath or affirmation. Proceed to fill out the Jurat.

**Sample of Oaths:**

**"Do you solemnly swear that the statements in this document are true and correct for all intents and purposes there unto pertaining, so help you God?"**
**"Do you swear that the statementsin this document are true, so help you God?"**

**Sample of Affirmations:**

**"Do you affirm that the statements contained in this document are true and correct for all intents and purposes?"**
**"Do you affirm that the statements in this document are true?"**

# AFFIDAVIT OF CITIZENSHIP
## (TEMPORARY USE ONLY– NOT A GOVERNMENT DOCUMENT)

FULL NAME RICHY (FIRST) — (MIDDLE) RICH (LAST)

DATE OF BIRTH MAY 5, 1940 TIME 2:00 (a.m.)/p.m. ☒ MALE ☐ FEMALE

PLACE OF BIRTH DESERT SPRINGS, ARIZONA CITIZEN OF UNITED STATE

STREET ADDRESS 4 DUSTY LANE

CITY, STATE, ZIP PENTEL, OREGON TELEPHONE 888-555-3333

NEAREST LIVING RELATIVE NONE RELATIONSHIP ______

STREET ADDRESS ______

CITY, STATE, ZIP ______ TELEPHONE ______

EMPLOYER'S NAME SEESAW MILLS OCCUPATION LUMBERJACK

STREET ADDRESS 8 FALLING TREES

CITY, STATE, ZIP PENTEL, OREGON TELEPHONE 999-333-5555

FATHER'S FULL NAME FATHER UNKNOWN OCCUPATION —

RESIDENCE AT TIME OF YOUR BIRTH —

AGE AT TIME OF YOUR BIRTH — BIRTHPLACE: —

MOTHER'S FULL NAME SELMA RICH OCCUPATION SECRETARY

RESIDENCE AT TIME OF YOUR BIRTH 22 APPLE ROAD, CORE, WASHINGTON

AGE AT TIME OF YOUR BIRTH 30 BIRTHPLACE: WASHINGTON STATE

STATE OF CALIFORNIA )
COUNTY OF ORANGE )

I, RICHY RICH, hereby swear or affirm that the facts and dates as alleged above are true and correct to the best of my knowledge and belief, and that I am a citizen of ______ or a naturalized citizen of THE UNITED STATES OF AMERICA

Richy Rich (SIGNED BY PRINCIPLE)

STATE OF CALIFORNIA
COUNTY OF ORANGE

On MAY 10, 2004 before me, NOTARY'S NAME personally appeared RICHY RICH ~~personally known to me~~ (or proved to me on the basis of satisfactory evidence) to be the person whose name is subscribed to the within instrument and acknowledged to me that he/~~she~~ executed the same in his/her authorized capacity, and that by his/~~her~~ signature on the instrument the person, or the entity upon behalf of which the person acted, executed the instrument. I CERTIFY UNDER PENALTY OF PERJURY UNDER THE LAWS OF THE STATE OF CALIFORNIA THAT THE FOREGOING PARAGRAPH IS TRUE AND CORRECT.

WITNESS my hand and official seal.

NOTARY SIGNATURE

# *SCENARIO 2*

## *"AFFIDAVIT OF CITIZENSHIP"*

Richy Rich calls you to have a document notarized. He is in the hospital. He states "I just had surgery 2 days ago and I have a document I need notarized." You ask him if he has a current valid ID with him and he says he does. Then you ask him, since he just had surgery, is he on any medication that would affect his judgment. He says he is on medication, but doesn't think its affecting his judgment. You tell him you will go to the hospital to see him in person, and I may have to talk to the nurse to be sure your judgment is not being affected before I can notarize the document.

When you arrive in Mr. Rich's room, the nurse just happens to be there. I introduce myself as a notary and tell her Mr. Rich has a document that needs to be signed and I need to ask you if he is on any medication that would affect his judgment? The nurse says "He's just on Tylenol and his judgment is fine." You thank her and have a conversation with Mr. Rich, to judge for yourself.

You fill out a one line item entry with Mr. Rich' s information in your Sequential Journal and under additional information write in the nurse's name and the questions you asked and the response you received.

You notice the document is an " Affidavit of Citizenship"; it has an Acknowledgment instruction on the bottom of the page. Those are the notary instructions. Just above that there's another statement, which Mr. Rich fills out himself and signs. Although it says he swears or affirms, you do not give him the oath or affirmation. The oath or affirmation is a separate part of the document that he completes himself.

Fill out and complete the Acknowledgment instruction portion only.

Since the Acknowledgement does not comply with 2008 wording you may attach a 2008 acknowledgement or you may cross out "Personally known to me" and write in "I certify etc."

Form R240 **LIMITED POWER OF ATTORNEY**

**(With Durable Provision)**

**TO ALL PERSONS**, be it known, that I, RICHY RICH
of GREENBACK, NEVADA
as Grantor, do hereby make and grant a limited and specific power of attorney to
of JUSTIN POOR
and appoint and constitute said individual as my attorney-in-fact.

My named attorney-in-fact shall have full power and authority to undertake, commit and perform only the following acts on my behalf to the same extent as if I had done so personally; all with full power of substitution and revocation in the presence: (Describe specific authority)

HANDLE ALL FINANCIAL ISSUES.

The authority granted shall include such incidental acts as are reasonably required or necessary to carry out and perform the specific authorities and duties stated or contemplated herein.

My attorney-in-fact agrees to accept this appointment subject to its terms, and agrees to act and perform in said fiduciary capacity consistent with my best interests as my attorney-in-fact deems advisable, and I thereupon ratify all acts so carried out.

I agree to reimburse my attorney-in-fact all reasonable costs and expenses incurred in the fulfillment of the duties and responsibilities enumerated herein.

**Special durable provisions:**

This power of attorney shall not be affected by disability of the Grantor. This power of attorney may be revoked by the Grantor giving notice of revocation to the attorney-in-fact, provided that any party relying in good faith upon this power of attorney shall be protected unless and until said party has either a) actual or constructive notice of revocation, or b) upon recording of said revocation in the public records where the Grantor resides.

**Other terms:**

NONE

Signed under seal this 5 th day of FEBRUARY , ~~19~~ 2003
Signed in the presence of:

______________________ Richy Rich
Witness Grantor

______________________ Justin Poor
Witness Attorney-in-Fact

STATE OF CALIFORNIA

COUNTY OF ORANGE

On FEBUARY 5, 2008 before me, NOTARIES NAME,
(Date) (Name and title of the officer)

personally appeared RICHY RICH ______________ ______________, who proved to me on the basis of
(Name of person signing)
satisfactory evidence to be the person~~(s)~~ whose name~~(s)~~ is~~/are~~ subscribed to the within instrument and acknowledged to me that he/she/they executed the same in his/her/their authorized capacity~~(ies)~~, and that by his~~/her/their~~ signature~~(s)~~ on the instrument the person~~(s)~~, or the entity upon behalf of which the person~~(s)~~ acted, executed the instrument.

I certify under PENALTY OF PERJURY under the laws of the State of California that the foregoing paragraph is true and correct.

WITNESS my hand and official seal.

SIGNED BY NOTARY
Signature of officer

* There are various types of homestead forms depending on each person's legal status. Before you use this form you many want to consult an

## *SCENARIO 3*

### *"LIMITED POWER OF ATTORNEY"*

Richey Rich is having surgery and he wants his friend Justin Poor to be his "Attorney in Fact" for a financial matter regarding the sale of his truck.

Mr. Rich comes to you and asks you to notarize his "Limited Power of Attorney". You ask to see his current valid ID and enter a one line item entry in your Sequential Journal.

If Mr. Rich already signed the document, just ask him if he acknowledges that it is his signature, he does not need to re-sign.

The Notary then fills out the Acknowledgment instructions on the "Power of Attorney"

NAME

STREET ADDRESS

CITY, STATE & ZIP CODE

SPACE ABOVE THIS LINE FOR RECORDER'S USE

# BILL OF SALE

The undersigned, RICHY RICH,

for a valuable consideration, receipt of which is hereby acknowledged, do___ sell to SELMA BUCKS

the personal property described as

2000 FORD TRUCK

The seller X do__, for heirs, executors, administrators and successors, covenant and agree to warrant and defend the title to the property hereby conveyed, against the just and lawful claims and demands of all persons whomsoever.

Dated:

AUGUST 2, 2003

RICHY RICH by
JUSTIN POOR - ATTORNEY IN FACT

STATE OF ______________________

COUNTY OF ______________________

On ____________ before me, ______________________
(NAME, TITLE OF OFFICER-I.E. "JANE DOE, NOTARY PUBLIC")

personally appeared ______________________

personally known to me (or proved to me on the basis of satisfactory evidence) to be the person(s) whose name(s) is/are subscribed to the within instrument and acknowledged to me that he/she/they executed the same in his/her/their authorized capacity(ies), and that by his/her/their signature(s) on the instrument the person(s), or the entity upon behalf of which the person(s) acted, executed the instrument.

WITNESS MY HAND AND OFFICIAL SEAL.

SEE ATTACHED ATTORNEY IN FACT ACK./INITIALS OF NOTARY
(SIGNATURE)
DATE (SEAL)

## *SCENARIO 4*

### *"BILL OF SALE"*

Richy Rich is having surgery and he asked his friend Justin Poor to be his "Attorney in Fact" for a financial matter that will be coming up. Richy Rich sold his 2000 Ford Truck and will need the "Bill of Sale" notarized while he's in the hospital.

Justin Poor comes to you and says he's the "Attorney in Fact" for Mr. Rich. He has a "Bill of Sale" that needs to be notarized. You ask to see the Power of Attorney. Mr. Poor forgot it at his home, that's OK, you don't need to see it, because you are notarizing the principal (Attorney in Fact) standing before you. (It's a good idea to see the Power of Attorney, if they have it, for expiration date and other information). You may still notarize the "Bill of Sale" because again, you're notarizing the person in front of you and he's signing as "Attorney in Fact", you are following the California State code.

Fill out a one line item entry in your Sequential Journal for Mr. Poor and fill out the "Attorney in Fact" loose leaf Acknowledgment form and attach to the back of the "Bill of Sale"

Notice how Mr. Poor signed Mr. Richy Rich's name and Mr. Poor signed his name and put "Attorney in Fact" next to it. The Notary did not use the standard Acknowledgment on the document. The Notary wrote on the bottom in the notary instruction, "see attached "Attorney in Fact" Acknowledgment, the notary initialed and dated the statement.

Note: If you do not have any loose leaf Attorney in Fact Acknowledgment Certificates, don't panic. You may use the Acknowledgment that is on the document. The Acknowledgment states "personally appeared", before you, which in this case is the Attorney in Fact.

(See procedures for filling out "Attorney in Fact" Acknowledgment in this handbook, page 38 and 39).

RECORDING REQUESTED BY

AND WHEN RECORDED MAIL TO:

NAME

STREET ADDRESS

CITY, STATE & ZIP CODE

SPACE ABOVE THIS LINE FOR RECORDER'S USE ONLY

# DECLARATION OF HOMESTEAD

I, JUSTIN POOR
(Full Name of Declarant)

do hereby certify and declare as follows:

(1) I hereby claim as a declared homestead the premises located in the City of HUNTINGTON BEACH

County of ORANGE, State of CALIFORNIA

commonly known as 619 BEACH ROAD
(Street Address)

and more particularly described as follows: [Give complete legal description]

SAND LOT, CORNER OF PEBBLES AND ROCK PILE

(2) I am the declared homestead owner of the above declared homestead.

(3) I own the following interest in the above declared homestead:

(4) The above declared homestead is [strike inapplicable clause] my principal dwelling and the principal dwelling of my spouse

[strike inapplicable clause] I am ~~my spouse is~~ currently residing on that declared homestead.

(5) The facts stated in this Declaration are true as of my personal knowledge.

JANUARY 2, 2002
Date

Justin Poor
(Signature of Declarant)

STATE OF CALIFORNIA

COUNTY OF ORANGE

On 1-02-08 (Date) before me, NAME OF NOTARY (Name and title of the officer), personally appeared JUSTIN POOR (Name of person signing), who proved to me on the basis of satisfactory evidence to be the person~~(s)~~ whose name~~(s)~~ ~~is/are~~ subscribed to the within instrument and acknowledged to me that he/~~she/they~~ executed the same in his/~~her/their~~ authorized capacity~~(ies)~~, and that by his/her/their signature(s) on the instrument the person~~(s)~~, or the entity upon behalf of which the person~~(s)~~ acted, executed the instrument.

I certify under PENALTY OF PERJURY under the laws of the State of California that the foregoing paragraph is true and correct.

WITNESS my hand and official seal.

SIGNATURE BY NOTARY
Signature of officer

(Seal)

* There are various types of homestead forms depending on each person's legal status. Before you use this form you many want to consult an

# SCENARIO 5

## *"DECLARATION OF HOMESTEAD"*

Justin Poor calls you stating he has a "Homestead Declaration" he needs notarized.

You ask if he has a current valid ID. He says "No, I've lost my identification". Let him know that when you arrive at his house, he must have 2 people that know him and they must have a current valid ID. (These are the 2 Credible Witnesses you will need to identify Mr. Poor).

When you arrive for your appointment, Mr. Poor has 2 of his friends and they have their current valid ID.

You enter a one line item entry in your Sequential Journal for each Credible Witness. Give each Credible Witness the oath or affirmation (see bottom of page for questions you ask for Credible Witnesses) and have them sign your Sequential Journal. Under additional information write out the questions you asked and the answers you were given while they were under oath or affirmation. (You do not charge the Credible Witnesses a fee).

If Mr. Poor already signed the document, ask him if he acknowledges that it is his signature on the document. It is not necessary for him to re-sign the document in your presence. Although, he must state that he did sign the document.

Enter a a one line item entry in your Sequential Journal for Mr. Poor and have him sign your Sequential Journal. Proceed to fill out the Acknowledgment instructions on the bottom of the form.

Note: You will have three – one line item entries – in your Sequential Journal.

**Oath or Affirmation for 2 Credible Witnesses:**
**Do you personally know the principal?**
**Answer: Must be Yes**
**Do you have any beneficial or financial interest or named in the document?**
**Answer: Must be No**
**Do you know the principal does not have an ID and is difficult for him to get one?**
**Answer: Must be Yes**
**Is the principal the same person named in the document?**
**Answer: Must be Yes**

Order No. @
Escrow No. @
Loan No. @

WHEN RECORDED MAIL TO:

@
@
@
@

DOCUMENTARY TRANSFER TAX $__________________ SPACE ABOVE THIS LINE FOR RECORDER'S USE

.....Computed on the consideration or value of property conveyed, OR

.....Computed on the consideration or value less liens or encumbrances remaining at time of sale

____________________________
Signature of Declarant or Agent determining tax - Firm Name

# GRANT DEED

FOR A VALUABLE CONSIDERATION, receipt of which is hereby acknowledged,

@ RICHY RICH

hereby GRANT(S) to

@, JUSTIN POOR

the real property in the City of @, County of @, State of California, described as

@ GOLDEN ACRES, GREENBACK, LOT 86, TRACK NUMBER 002, MAP BOOK 1666, PAGE NO. 21, COUNTY OF GREENBACK

Dated @

6-3-04

Richy Rich
@

@

@

@

STATE OF CALIFORNIA }
COUNTY OF GREENBACK }ss

On 3-16-08 before me,
NOTARY PUBLICS NAME,
a notary public, personally appeared
RICHY RICH,

proved to me on the basis of satisfactory evidence to be the person~~(s)~~ whose name~~(s)~~ is/~~are~~ subscribed to the within instrument and acknowledged to me that he/~~she/they~~ executed the same in his/~~her/their~~ authorized capacity~~(ies)~~, and that by his/~~her/their~~ signature~~(s)~~ on the instrument the person~~(s)~~ or the entity upon behalf of which the person~~(s)~~ acted, executed the instrument. I certify under PENALTY OF PERJURY under the laws of the State of California that the foregoing paragraph is true and correct.

WITNESS my hand and official seal.

Signature SIGNED BY NOTARY

**MAIL TAX STATEMENTS TO:**
@

# *SCENARIO 6*

### *"GRANT DEED"*

Mr. Richy Rich asks you to notarize a Grant Deed.

You ask him if he has a current valid ID, he does not. Mr. Rich was given your name from a mutual friend, Jane Smith. Mr. Rich brought along Jane Smith to serve as his Credible Witness

You, the notary, knows Jane Smith and she presented a proper ID, and Jane Smith knows Richy Rich. If Mr. Rich already signed the document, just ask him if he acknowledges that it is his signature. It is not necessary for him to re-sign the document in your presence.

The notary enters a one line item entry in your Sequential Journal for Jane Smith as a Credible Witness. Give Jane Smith the oath or affirmation (see bottom of page for questions you ask for Credible Witnesses) and have her sign your Sequential Journal. Under additional information write out the questions you asked and the answers you received for putting her under the oath or affirmation. (You never charge anything for Credible Witnesses-your entry under fee should be $0.00.)

You enter a one line item entry in your Sequential Journal for Mr. Rich and have him sign your Sequential Journal. Proceed to fill out he Acknowledgment instructions on the bottom of the form for Mr. Rich.

Note: You will have two – one line item entries – in your Sequential Journal.

**Oath or Affirmation for 1 Credible Witnesses:**

**Do you personally know the principal?**
**Answer: Must be Yes**
**Do you have any beneficial or financial interest or named in the document?**
**Answer: Must be No**
**Do you know the principal does not have an ID and is difficult for him to get one?**
**Answer: Must be Yes**
**Is the principal the same person named in the document?**
**Answer: Must be Yes**

## ACKNOWLEDGMENT OF SERVICE
## AND ASSENT TO PROBATE INSTANTER

GEORGIA, ____CHATHAM____ COUNTY

IN RE: PETITION OF ROBERT B. JONES JR. TO PROBATE THE WILL OF PATTY JONES, DECEASED, IN SOLEMN FORM

We, the undersigned, being over 18 years of age, laboring under no legal disability and being heirs of the above-named decedent, hereby acknowledge service of a copy of the petition to probate said will in solemn form, purported will, and notice, waive copies of same, waive further service and notice, and hereby assent to the probate of said will in solemn form without further delay.

SIGNATURE(S) OF HEIRS

Sworn to and subscribed before
me this ____ day of ________,20__.

ROBERT B. JONES JR.

NOTARY/CLERK OF PROBATE COURT

---

STATE OF: CALIFORNIA
COUNTY OF: ORANGE

Sworn to and subscribed before
me this 2 day of JUNE ,2004, BY BETTY JONES

Betty Jones
BETTY JONES

SIGNED BY NOTARY
NOTARY/CLERK OF PROBATE COURT
SATISFACTORILY I.D.

Sworn to and subscribed before
me this ____ day of ________,20__.

NOTARY/CLERK OF PROBATE COURT

---

Sworn to and subscribed before
me this ____ day of ________,20__.

JAMES JONES

NOTARY/CLERK OF PROBATE COURT

# *SCENARIO 7*

## *"ACKNOWLEDGMENT OF SERVICE AND ASSENT TO PROBATE INSTANTER"*

Betty Jones, whom you personally know, and provided a required I.D. comes to you with a document from Georgia. Her mother passed away and she needs to notarize this document and send it back the next day so her other siblings can sign it.

If the principal(s) signed the document before they brought it to you they must resign the document in front of you. Fill out one line item in your Sequential Journal, have the principal sign your book, and give her the oath or affirmation. Proceed to fill out the Jurat.

Note: If you notice on the top of this document the venue is from Georgia, do not change that to California, because that is part of the document. (Remember you never change anything on a document – only on the notaries instructions are you allowed to write or change anything.) See how the venue was placed next to the "Sworn to and subscribed before" on the side of the notaries instructions.

Notice in the title of this document it states "Acknowledgment" although the Notary Instructions are actually for a Jurat Service. ALWAYS follow the Notary Instructions. As illustrated in the example, the Notary Seal covered printed matter. You will have to fill out a loose leaf Jurat Certificate and next to your seal write "see attached loose leaf Jurat Certificate", initial, and date.

***Sample of Oaths:***

***"Do you solemnly swear that the statements in this document are true and correct for all intents and purposes there unto pertaining, so help you God?"***
***"Do you swear that the statements in this document are true, so help you God?"***

***Sample of Affirmations: "Do you affirm that the statements contained in this document are true and correct for all intents andpurposes?"***
***"Do you affirm that the statements in this document are true?"***

# AFFIDAVIT OF BIRTH

PERSONAL AND STATISTICAL PARTICULARS ABOUT CHILD

Full name of child LESLIE JONES

Date of birth MAY 2, 2002 At 1:00 A.M. P.M. Sex FEMALE

Place of Birth NOME, ALASKA

PERSONAL AND STATISTICAL PARTICULARS ABOUT CHILD'S FATHER

Full name of father JOHN JONES

Residence at child's birth 4 DOGSLED ROAD, NOME, ALASKA

Age at child's birth 30 years. Color or race CAUCASIAN

Birthplace OZ, KANSAS

Occupation at child's birth DOGSLED TRAINER

PERSONAL AND STATISTICAL PARTICULARS ABOUT CHILD'S MOTHER

Full maiden name of mother BETTY BOOP

Residence at child's birth 4 DOGSLED ROAD, NOME, ALASKA

Age at child's birth 29 years. Color or race CAUCASIAN

Birthplace NOME, ALASKA

Occupation at child's birth DOGSLED TRAINER

This is the FIRST child born to this mother.

Including this child, there were then 0 children of this mother living.

STATE OF CALIFORNIA }
County of ORANGE } ss.

I hereby certify that I am the FATHER & MOTHER of the above mentioned child and that the facts and date as alleged are true and correct to the best of my knowledge and belief and that ~~I am~~ WERE a native citizen of THE UNITED STATES OF AMERICA
(CROSS OUT THE WORDS THAT DO NOT APPLY)

a citizen through naturalization of THE UNITED STATES OF AMERICA

John Jones and Betty Jones
AFFIANT

ADDRESS

SUBSCRIBED AND SWORN TO before me on JUNE 3, 2003, By John Jones AND BETTY JONES, SATISFACTORILY I.D.

SIGNED BY NOTARY

Notary Public in and for said State.
STATE OF CALIFORNIA, COUNTY OF ORANGE

## *SCENARIO 8*
### *"AFFIDAVIT OF BIRTH"*

Mr. and Mrs. Jones come to you with a completed "Affidavit of Birth" document for you to notarize.

This form has Jurat instructions. You personally know Mr. and Mrs. Jones, and they provided a required I.D.You enter in your Sequential Journal a one line item entry each for Mr. Jones and Mrs. Jones, the principals. Administer the oath or affirmation to both.

Please look at this form carefully-notice half way down where it says "State of: and County of: the principals fill that part out and sign their names where it says "affiant". If they signed it before they brought to you they have to resign it in front of you.

Your Jurat instructions begin where it says "Subscribed and Sworn to: there is no venue area in your instruction, so just put them on the bottom or top of the notarial instructions where they will fit.

If there is no room to write in "Proved to me on the basis of satisfactory evidence to be the person(s) who appeared before me" attach a loose leaf Jurat Certificate.

**...Another Sample of an Oath:**

**"Do you solemnly swear that the statements in this document are true and correct for all intents and purposes there unto pertaining, so help you God?"**
**"Do you swear that the statements in this document are true, so help you God?"**

**...Another Sample of an Affirmation:**

**"Do you affirm that the statements contained in this document are true and correct for all intents and purposes?"**
**"Do you affirm that the statements in this document are true?"**

RECORDING REQUESTED BY

AND WHEN RECORDED MAIL TO:

NAME

STREET ADDRESS

CITY, STATE & ZIP CODE

Title Order No. ____________ Escrow or Loan No. ____________

SPACE ABOVE THIS LINE FOR RECORDER'S USE

# REVOCATION OF POWER OF ATTORNEY

TO WHOM IT MAY CONCERN:

On FEB. 5, 2003, I, RICHY RICH, a resident of GREENBACK County, State of NEVADA executed a Power of Attorney appointing JUSTIN POOR my attorney in fact to perform certain acts for me.

On FEB. 29, 2003, said Power of Attorney was recorded in the Office of the Recorder of GREENBACK County, State of NEVADA, as Instrument No. 619, in Book 925, Page 1029.

I HEREBY REVOKE said Power of Attorney, and all powers therein granted to my said attorney in fact.

WITNESS my hand this SEPTEMBER day of 25, 2003.

Richy Rich

Betty Jones

AS SUBSCRIBING WITNESS

STATE OF ____________________

COUNTY OF ____________________

On ____________ before me, ______________________________
(NAME, TITLE OF OFFICER-I.E. "JANE DOE, NOTARY PUBLIC")

______________________________ personally appeared

personally known to me (or proved to me on the basis of satisfactory evidence) to be the person(s) whose name(s) is/are subscribed to the within instrument and acknowledged to me that he/she/they executed the same in his/her/their authorized capacity(ies), and that by his/her/their signature(s) on the instrument the person(s), or the entity upon behalf of which the person(s) acted, executed the instrument.
WITNESS MY HAND AND OFFICIAL SEAL.

SEE ATTACHED SUBSCRIBING WITNESS ACK.
(SIGNATURE)

WOLCOTTS FORM 1404 - Rev. 4-94
POWER OF ATTORNEY - REVOCATION
(price class 3A)

©1994 WOLCOTTS FORMS, INC.

Before you use this form, fill in all blanks, and make whatever changes are appropriate and necessary to your particular transaction. Consult a lawyer if you doubt the form's fitness for your purpose and use. Wolcotts makes no representation or warranty, express or implied, with respect to the merchantability or fitness of this form for an intended use or purpose.

# *SCENARIO 9*

## *"REVOCATION OF POWER OF ATTORNEY"*

Your friend of 10 years, Richy Rich comes to you with a document that a friend of his Betty Jones needs to have notarized. Richy Rich told her that he has to leave on an emergency trip out of the country. Would she mind having the document notarized. Richy Rich signed the document in front of his friend Betty, and had her sign the document also. Betty also brought with her a friend of hers, Toby who also knows you, the notary to be used as a credible witness, who must provide a proper ID.
Betty Jones comes to you, because she knows you're a Notary, and you (the Notary) and Betty, are long time friends. Betty tells you of the above circumstances. The Notary proceeds to fill out a one line item in her Sequential Journal, listing Betty as a Subscribing Witness and on another line Toby as credible witness.

The Notary puts the Subscribing Witness under oath or affirmation and asks the following questions. (See subscribing witness for oath.) The Notary also puts the credible witness under oath (see credible witness for oath). In the additional information part of the journal write down the questions and answers you received when you put her under oath or affirmation

The Subscribing Witness Betty Jones will sign her own name in your Sequential Journal. If the Subscribing Witness has not signed the document under the principal's name have her do so. You as the notary <u>will not</u> put any information requiring the ID of the Subscribing Witness, because you personally know the Subscribing Witness, Betty Jones.

**REMEMBER: THE NOTARY <u>MAY NOT</u> NOTARIZE A DOCUMENT FOR A SUBSCRIBING WITNESS IF IT IS A:**

- ***QUITCLAIM DEED,***
- ***GRANT DEED***
- ***MORTGAGE,***
- ***SECURITY AGREEMENT***
- ***DEED OF TRUST***

**Note: All the above items listed involve Real Property. (California State Code / Civil Code Section #1195)**

Please see "Subscribing Witness" loose leaf certificate for instructions on how to fill out the certificate.

RECORDING REQUESTED BY

AND WHEN RECORDED MAIL TO:

NAME

STREET ADDRESS

CITY, STATE & ZIP CODE

Title Order No. ____________ Escrow or Loan No. ____________

SPACE ABOVE THIS LINE FOR RECORDER'S USE

# RELEASE OF MECHANIC'S LIEN

The Mechanic's Lien claimed by RAY GAMBLE AND PAULINE GAMBLE
(NAME OF PERSON OR FIRM AS IT APPEARS ON MECHANIC'S LIEN)

against CRACKED PIPE PLUMBING
(OWNER OR PURPORTED OWNER AND/OR CONTRACTOR AS NAMED IN MECHANIC'S LIEN)

and claiming a lien upon that certain real property located in the County of ORANGE, State of CALIF, and described as follows: TRACT A, LOT 10, PARCEL 210

(DESCRIPTION OF PROPERTY WHERE THE WORK AND/OR MATERIALS WERE FURNISHED. ALTHOUGH THE STREET ADDRESS IS SUFFICIENT, IT IS ADVISABLE TO GIVE BOTH THE STREET ADDRESS AND THE LEGAL DESCRIPTION.)

is hereby released, the claim thereunder having been fully paid and satisfied, and that certain Mechanic's Lien, dated MAY 10, 2003 and recorded as Instrument No. 926 on MAY 7, 2003 in Book 51, Page 110, Official Records of ORANGE County, State of CA, is hereby satisfied and discharged.

Dated: JUNE 1, 2003

Firm Name: Ray Gamble and Pauline Gamble
(AS IT APPEARS ON MECHANIC'S LIEN)

By: ____________

STATE OF CALIFORNIA

COUNTY OF ORANGE

On JANUARY 1, 2008 (Date) before me, NOTARIES NAME (Name and title of the officer)

personally appeared RAY GAMBLE (Name of person signing), who proved to me on the basis of satisfactory evidence to be the person(s) whose name(s) is/are subscribed to the within instrument and acknowledged to me that he/she/they executed the same in his/her/their authorized capacity(ies), and that by his/her/their signature(s) on the instrument the person(s) or the entity upon behalf of which the person(s) acted, executed the instrument.

I certify under PENALTY OF PERJURY under the laws of the State of California that the foregoing paragraph is true and correct.

WITNESS my hand and official seal.

SIGNED BY NOTARY
Signature of officer

* There are various types of homestead forms depending on each person's legal status. Before you use this form you many want to consult an

# SCENARIO 10

## "RELEASE OF MECHANIC'S LIEN"

Ray and Pauline Gamble came to you to have a "Release of Mechanic's lien" signed.

You ask them for their ID and Mr. Gamble hands you his current driver's license. However, Mrs. Gamble is in the process of applying for a new driver's license. (Mrs. Gamble's license was stolen along with her wallet and winnings from her "Texas Hold'em Poker" tournament). She stated she may receive her new license in the mail this week. She has to leave for work and doesn't have time to find two Credible Witnesses.

You suggest that you can notarize Mr. Gamble's signature today and have him call you when Mrs. Gamble receives her new license. He says that's a great idea – so you notarize his signature. Fill out a one line item entry in your Sequential Journal for Mr. Gamble only.

He calls you the next day and states that his wife received her replacement driver's license and is now prepared to have the notarization done.

The process will require you to have her sign the document and attach a loose leaf Acknowledgment Certificate to the back of the document, since her portion of the notary process was done after the original notary process.

Fill out a one line item entry in your Sequential Journal for Mrs. Gamble.

*THIS PAGE LEFT BLANK INTENTIONALLY*

# ***PRACTICAL INFORMATION REGARDING*** THE LOAN SIGNING PROCESS

***DESIGNED AS A REFERENCE TOOL TO BE USED BY THE RECENTLY COMMISSIONED OR EXPERIENCED CALIFORNIA NOTARY PUBLIC***

**COPYRIGHT © 2004 - 2009 ALL RIGHTS RESERVED**
**Co-authored by: Stephanie Hulme and Susan M. Allen**
**Commissioned California Notaries**

# A BRIEF DESCRIPTION OF COMMON LOAN SIGNING DOCUMENTS

***THE FOLLOWING IS A DESCRIPTION OF SOME COMMON DOCUMENTS USED FOR THE LOAN SIGNING PROCESS:***

***Please note: These documents may or may not be included in the package you are processing. Every package is different. This is information of some general, common documents used in the industry that you should be aware of.***

1. **APPLICATION DISCLOSURE:**
   The mortgage lender or broker is required to inform the borrower of some of the fees that will be charged in connection with their application of a loan. IE: Application Fee, Appraisal Fee, Credit Report Fee, etc. etc.

2. **APPRAISAL DISCLOSURE:**
   This form indicates you have the right to a copy of the appraisal report used in connection with your application for credit.

3. **APPRAISAL DISCLOSURE:**
   This form indicates you have the right to a copy of the appraisal report used in connection with your application for credit.

4. **BORROWER'S CERTIFICATION AND AUTHORIZATION:**
   A certification saying the information on the loan application has not changed, and there have been no misrepresentations on any other document.

5. **CLOSING INSTRUCTIONS:**
   These are to be signed by the "CLOSING AGENT" not the Notary Public. If this document is not signed by the time you processing the loan documents, leave it blank, and go to the next document. It does not need to be signed by the borrower(s) or the Notary Public.

6. **COMPLIANCE AGREEMENT:**
   **Notarizations are usually required.**
   The borrower(s) agree to cooperate and adjust for clerical errors, any or all loan closing documents, if deemed necessary.

7. **CONFIDENTIAL STATEMENT OF INFORMATION:**
   When filled out it will be compared by the title company for similarity of name affecting the property ownership.

# A BRIEF DESCRIPTION OF COMMON LOAN SIGNING DOCUMENTS

*Continued*

***COMMON DOCUMENTS USED FOR THE LOAN PROCESS:***

8. **CONFIDENTIAL STATEMENT OF INFORMATION:**
   When filled out it will be compared by the title company for similarity of name affecting the property ownership.

9. **CUSTOMER IDENTIFICATION VERIFICATION:**
   Important information regarding procedures for opening a new account. Verifies the identification used by the Notary Public for processing of the documents. (*Note: The notary public fills this document out and signs it where indicated. Also requires your title – "Notary Public". Notarization is not required*).

10. **DEED OF TRUST:**
    **Notarization is required, and if indicated to do so, initials are required.**
    Be sure to scan the document for placement of initials, if they are required.
    Shows principal(s) name on title of property.
    Will indicate legal description and/or property address.
    All persons on the Deed must sign exactly as their name appears.

11. **ERRORS AND OMISSIONS COMPLIANCE AGREEMENT:**
    **Notarizations are usually required.**
    Allows documents to be corrected by the lender after they have been signed by the borrower(s).

12. **ESCROW INSTRUCTIONS:**
    These are instructions from the lender to the escrow company. They are usually only initialed by the borrower(s) on the bottom left.

13. **EVIDENCE OF JOINT APPLICATION:**
    The intent to apply for joint credit.

14. **FEDERAL EQUAL CREDIT OPPORTUNITY ACT NOTICE:**
    This form is usually in every loan package. It prohibits creditors from discriminating against credit applicants on the basis of race, color, religion, national origin, sex, marital status, and age.

# A BRIEF DESCRIPTION OF COMMON LOAN SIGNING DOCUMENTS

*Continued*

***COMMON DOCUMENTS USED FOR THE LOAN PROCESS:***

15. **FEDERAL TRUTH IN LENDING DISCLOSURE STATEMENT:**
    Disclosure of the annual percentage rate to borrower(s) and total loan amount. Also listed will be the Annual Percentage Rate (APR), Finance Charge, Amount Financed, Total of Payments, Total Sale Price, Late Charge, Pre-payment Penalty (if any), and Signed And Dated by the Document Signer.

16. **FIRST PAYMENT NOTICE:**
    It gives the borrower the information on how much their payment will be and where to send the payment.

17. **FLOOD CERTIFICATE:**
    Tells the borrower whether or not their property is in a flood zone.

18. **GOOD FAITH ESTIMATE OF SETTLEMENT CHARGES:**
    Estimate of the closing costs of the loan. It will indicate itemization of the amount financed. It is dated and signed by the borrower(s).

19. **HAZARD INSURANCE REQUIREMENTS NOTICE:**
    **Notarization may or may not be required**.
    Policies and procedures for minimum requirements for Hazard Insurance the lender requires of the borrower.

20. **HUD (U.S. DEPARTMENT OF HOUSING AND URBAN DEVELOPMENT**

    Estimate of all charges.
    Disclosure of the total loan amount. Also listed will be the Amount Financed, Settlement Charges, Taxes, Deposits, Notary Fees, and a number of other charges, or credits, pertaining to the specific loan.
    Probably will be in every set of loan documents.
    May or may not require signature.

21. **IMPOUND AUTHORIZATION:**
    Impound account is a fund created for insurance, taxes, and other expenses relating to the security property.
    Usually, requires signature and date.

# A BRIEF DESCRIPTION OF COMMON LOAN SIGNING DOCUMENTS

*Continued*

***COMMON DOCUMENTS USED FOR THE LOAN PROCESS:***

22. **IMPOUND AUTHORIZATION:**
    Impound account is a fund created for insurance, taxes, and other expenses relating to the security property.
    Usually, requires signature and date.

23. **LOAN SERVICING DISCLOSURE STATEMENT:**
    This disclosure statement is to make you aware the lender may sell or transfer your loan to a new provider.
    Usually signed by the borrower(s) and dated.

24. **NOTE:**
    Notarization (sometimes) and initials only required if instructed to do so.
    A written promise to pay a certain sum of money at a certain time.

25. **RIGHT OF RESCISSION – NOTICE OF RIGHT TO CANCEL:**
    This form applies to refinance loans only.
    Gives the borrower(s) 3 days (ending at midnight on the third day) to cancel the loan after they have signed the documents without penalties.
    If the Notary Public calculates the dates, it is the borrower who writes the rescission date on the document. (Make sure they also write the date on the copy you are going to leave with the borrower(s)).
    Remember that Sundays and Federal Holidays do not count in the calculation of the 3 day total. Business days counted are Monday through Saturday. For your accurate calculation of the rescission date, we recommended that you purchase a "Rescission Calendar".

26. **NOTICE OF RIGHT TO RECEIVE A COPY OF APPRAISAL:**
    Most copies of appraisals are attached to the borrower(s) copies of the loan.

27. **OCCUPANCY CERTIFICATE/AFFIDAVIT;**
    **Notarization is usually required, but not always**.
    Borrower(s) indicate if the property is the Principal Residence, Second Home, or an Investment Property.

*Continued*

## *COMMON DOCUMENTS USED FOR THE LOAN PROCESS:*

28. **PAYMENT LETTER TO BORROWER:**

This document informs the borrower(s) the date the loan starts, and the date the loan ends. It itemizes what the monthly payment consist of.

29. **PROPERTY OWNER'S AFFIDAVIT:**

**Notarization is usually required, but not always**.
This affidavit states the property has no leans, judgments, or law suits, etc.

30. **REQUEST FOR COPY OF TAX RETURNS:**

This document is used in the event that a copy of the borrower(s) tax return is needed.

31. **REQUEST FOR TAXPAYER IDENTIFICATION NUMBER:**

Each borrower will have his/her own form to sign.
This form is usually signed in the middle of the page.

32. **SIGNATURE AFFIDAVIT / AKA (ALSO KNOWN AS) STATEMENT:**

**Notarizations are required**.
The borrower(s) must sign their name as it appears on each line. They may have more than one legal name and must sign their name for each variation.

33. **TRUTH IN LENDING:**

Disclosure of the annual percentage rate to borrower(s) and total loan amounts.

# *WHAT THE "HECK" DO YOU DO?*

# *FROM START TO FINISH...*

## THE LOAN SIGNING SPECIALIST ASSIGNMENT

A. Title or Signing Company Calls:

- Negotiate payment
- Agree to loan signing
- How will you receive initial information sheet? Fax E-mail Pick up documents from an office
- How will the documents arrive and to whom?

B. Initial information sheet should contain the following:

- If appointment has been set with the borrower(s) or do you make arrangements for the appointment.
- Name of the document signer(s).
- Work, home, cell phone numbers of document(s) signers.
- Address of borrower(s) signing location.

**C.** Call Borrower(s) **Immediately**

- Confirm or make appointment with the borrower(s).
- Confirm all their phone numbers and give them yours.
- Ask if they have current valid ID, (if they don't arrange at this time for them to have 2 Credible Witnesses available with their current valid ID at the time of the borrower(s) signing.)
- If the borrower(s) have the loan documents, ask them if their names on the documents are spelled correctly, if not call the signing agency for further instructions. (If you have the loan documents please reference Letter D bullet #5 on page 73.)
- If the borrower(s) have the loan documents, ask them if their names match their ID, if not, now is the time to arrange for the 2 Credible Witnesses.

## THE LOAN SIGNING SPECIALIST ASSIGNMENT

***Continued***

D. Documents: If you receive them.

- Read notary instructions. Do the borrower(s) owe money at the time of signing, if so they need to have the check ready? Do the borrower(s) need copies of insurance forms, driver licenses, etc. to send back with the loan documents? Do you need to fax back a copy of any of the loan documents, before you mail them back? Do you need to call and leave a message that the signing was completed?
- You will receive 2 complete sets of loan documents, (one marked COPY and the original documents to be signed and sent back).
- Go through the original set of loan documents and put on signer stickers where the documents need to be signed and/or notarized.
- Most documents arrive from the lender already highlighted for signatures, initials, and notarizations.

**DO NOT USE A HIGHLIGHTER OR MARK ON ANY DOCUMENT, ANYTIME...**

- When you received the loan documents check the borrowers name to make sure it matches their ID. (When you called the borrowers to confirm their appointment ask them to get out their ID and read it to you over the phone so you can verify it matches. If it doesn't match, this is the time to call the signing company and ask for instructions or if you need to get 2 Credible Witnesses).

E. ARRIVE ON TIME...

- Introduce yourself (BE FRIENDLY, NICE & PROFESSIONAL).
- Sit at a dining room or kitchen table.
- If they offer you something to drink or eat, please decline without offending them.
- Have the borrower(s) sit across from you (so you control the documents.)
- Put the borrower(s) copy aside; don't give to them until you leave.
- Lay out your notary supplies.

## *WHAT THE "HECK" DO YOU DO?*

## *FROM START TO FINISH...*

### THE LOAN SIGNING SPECIALIST ASSIGNMENT

***Continued***

F. Inform the borrower(s) you are a notary and you are there just to "witness and identify" them. If they have any questions regarding their loan, please have the borrower(s) call their lender.

G. Ask for their ID.

- Fill out your Sequential Journal with their ID information.
- If you are using 2 Credible Witnesses put their ID information in your Sequential Journal and administer the oath or affirmation to them. (The Credible Witnesses do not need to stay for the complete signing process, they are only there to initially ID the borrower(s).

H. Remember, you control the loan documents. Place the loan documents in front of you. Place the top document in front of the first borrower/signer, show him where to initial or sign. Then place the document in front of the second borrower/signer, instruct them to initial or sign. Place the documents face down and continue through the rest of the loan documents so they stay in the same order you received them. This is very important.

REMEMBER...

*THEY MUST SIGN THEIR NAME AS IT IS TYPED ON THE DOCUMENT.*

I. Notarized the documents that need to be notarized as soon as the borrower(s) have signed them. Instruct them to sign your Sequential Journal and thumbprint, if required.

J. When all of the loan documents have been **Initialed, Signed and Notarized** review all the loan documents one by one to make sure...

- All names are signed correctly – using the exact name on the documents.
- All documents requiring dates are dated.
- All documents requiring initials are in the proper place.
- "Right of Rescission" has been executed properly.
- Information collected from the borrower, as requested by lender.

# *WHAT THE "HECK" DO YOU DO?*

## *FROM START TO FINISH...*
## THE LOAN SIGNING SPECIALIST ASSIGNMENT

***Continued***

K. Check your Sequential Journal and make sure all the required notarizations have been done correctly. Be sure that the borrower(s) have signed your Sequential Journal on all line item entries and thumbprints when required.

L. Put the signed documents and required items to be sent back in the envelope provided for you. Put away all of your notary supplies.

M. Give the "copy" of the loan documents to the borrower(s), thank them for their hospitality and leave.

N. Drop off the loan documents at the designated drop box or if you picked them up from an office return them where instructed.

***CONGRATULATIONS!***

***YOU JUST EARNED YOUR LOAN SIGNING SPECIALIST FEE!***

## *SAMPLE OF SIGNER OR CLOSER CHECK LIST*
## *LOAN CLOSING REQUEST*

***The following is a generic illustration of what a Loan Signing Specialist would be faxed from the signing or title company – for your reference.***

**"Stephanie and Sue's Signing Services"**

**8941 Atlanta Avenue #250**
**Huntington Beach, CA 92646**

**RE: Richy Rich ORDER #123456**
**LOCATION: 123 PARADISE LANE, CITY: FANTASYLAND, CA 98765**
**CLOSING DATE: JUNE 22, 2001 TIME: 12:30 P.M.**
**FEE: $125.00 PLEASE FOLLOW THE INSTRUCTIONS BELOW**
**PHONE: (H) 714.555.5555 (W) 949.555.4444**

### SIGNER OR CLOSER CHECK LIST

**THE FOLLOWING CONDITIONS MUST BE MET IN ORDER FOR FUNDS TO DISBURSE:**

1. **REVIEW HUD! If you are required to collect funds at closing, they must be certified and made payable to John Doe Title Company.**
2. **Obtain borrower's signatures, notarize documents, and initial where needed.**
3. **Fax a signed copy of the HUD Settlement sheet to John Doe Title Company at 949.555.9876**
4. **Please pick up insurance information.**
5. **Make sure the borrowers sign each document exactly as their names appear on each document.**
6. **If they have an AKA, they must sign their former name, AKA, and their current name.**

**PLEASE OVERNIGHT THE ENTIRE PACKAGE OF THE EXECUTED DOCUMENTS, INCLUDING THE HUD, TO: ADDRESSED FED EX ENVELOPE ENCLOSED Please call with your loan status upon completion of closing, and fax this invoice with the FedEx tracking number to: 949.555.9876.**

***THIS FORM FAXED BACK WITH TRACKING NUMBER*** WILL SERVE AS YOUR INVOICE!

## THINGS TO CONSIDER WHEN NEGOTIATING YOUR LOAN SIGNING FEE

For general information purposes, we must tell you that there will be certain situations that you will not be able to negotiate your fee. This is particularly true when you are working for a "loan signing" company. They will call you to tell you what they have available, when the loan signing is to take place, and how much they will pay you. At that time, you will accept or decline the assignment.
The following questions will assist you in calculating what you should charge for your loan signing fee.

***The number of loans the borrower(s) will have? (There could be multiple).***

***Will the borrower(s) be at the same address?***

***Address where the signing will take place. (It will not always be at the borrower(s) address).***

***If you are picking up the documents, where? Will you be returning them in person, if so, that's more time you need to allow for.***

***How many miles will you be traveling?***

***How long do you anticipate the signing to take, rule of thumb plan approximately one hour per signing, plus travel time?***

Take into consideration all of the above information – your time and mileage, with this information you can determine a reasonable fee. You can compare that to what you are offered, and make an informed decision.

Do not make the mistake of allowing your "ego" to direct your financial position. If you do, you can be guaranteed of one thing…you won't have one. You must build your experience and trust with any company you work for, before you can reap a higher financial reward.

# THINGS TO REMEMBER FOR LOAN SIGNING

1. Make sure the borrower(s) sign their name <u>exactly</u> as it appears on the loan documents.

   **i.e. Richy L. Rich not Richy Rich**

   The lenders want them to sign with their middle initial if the middle initial is on the loan documents. You may watch the borrower(s) sign the document and make sure it's done correctly. Most of the time borrower(s) have a certain way of signing their name, for instance, just their first initial and last name. All loan documents are drawn up with their complete name. The lenders want their complete signature. If it's done incorrectly the loan documents will need to be re-drawn and they could loose their rate lock. Not a good thing to have happen!
2. Check the dates on the loan documents. The borrowers *<u>may not sign</u>* before the printed date on the documents. However, they may sign anytime after the printed date on the documents, if the signing or title company approves it. **<u>DO NOT PRE-DATE OR POST-DATE THE LOAN DOCUMENTS</u>**
3. Make sure your notary stamp has ink. When stamping, be sure the impression is not smeared. The borders of the stamp cannot touch the sides of the document or touch any printed matter. This also applies to any notary process you do, not just loan document processing.
4. Always pay attention to your order sheets from lenders or signing companies. Read their instructions carefully and execute fully. If you work for the same company most of the time, don't assume your instructions are going to be the same every time. Each loan is different - for instance, sometimes the property address and the signing location are not the same.
5. You may have received the loan documents first, or they may be in the hands of the borrower(s). Regardless, you should always take a few minutes to look at the "Estimated Closing Statement" (line #1602) to see if a balance is due from the borrower(s). If there is a balance due, make sure you ask the borrower(s) for the check before you leave. If the borrower(s) cannot or won't provide a check, then have the borrower(s) put a Post-it note on the statement indicating why they did not provide a check.

# THINGS TO REMEMBER FOR LOAN SIGNING

*Continued*

6. If there are any documents that have been highlighted by the lender for information to be filled in, make sure the borrower(s) input the information needed. Again, if they don't have the information on hand or they already provided it, then have the borrower(s) put a Post-it note on the document. The reason the borrower(s) put a Post-it note on the document is to show the lender you did not forget your instructions. This places the responsibility on the borrower(s).

7. "Right of Rescission" date. If there is no date, you need to fill in the date. If the date is incorrect, cross out the incorrect date, fill in the correct date, and always have the borrower(s) initial the change. Be sure and get the Right of Rescission out of the borrower(s) "copy" of documents for the borrower(s) and write in the corrected date and have the borrower(s) initial the changes. Remember "business days" are Monday through Saturday. When calculating the rescission date, always exclude major holidays. Refer to your rescission calendar. (Right of Rescission is primarily used if you are re-financing).
8. Some lenders might include a "Right of Rescission" receipt or acknowledgment of receipt. The borrower(s) do sign this, but it is not dated. It just informs the borrower(s) the three days have lapsed and they have not cancelled their loan.

9. Remember, as a notary you are only responsible for identifying the borrower(s) and witnessing their signature. Always refer questions regarding their loan to the borrower(s) loan agent or broker. If the borrower(s) ask you where to find information on the document you may certainly show them. You never explain documents to the borrower(s), even if you're an expert in that particular field.

10. If for some reason you are running late, please call the borrower(s) and let them know your new arrival time. A good rule would be if you are going to be more than 10 minutes late.

11. When you leave the signing, always write down the tracking number of the return package. The lender will probably want the information on the sign off sheet you fax back. Lenders do not tolerate documents not being returned promptly. This part of the process is just as important as signing the loan documents.

12. As a loan signing specialist, you are responsible for all California State mandated rules and regulations pertaining to the notarial act. That does not change under any circumstances.

13. Beware of any company that asks you to do anything other than what you know to be proper and correct with regard to California State Law. i.e.: If they ask you to pre-date or post-date the document.

14. It's important to represent the lender or signing company in a professional and knowledgeable manner. Having a good understanding of the loan documents allows you to present yourself in a confident manner.

15. Always dress appropriately. No jeans, t-shirts, or sandals. Remember you may be the only individual they will have personal contact with, throughout the loan process. Be professional.

16. The Notary/Loan Signing Specialist should avoid the "3 W's"...

**WHAT, WHEN, and WHY**

- **i.e.: WHAT IS MY PENALTY FOR PREPAYMENT**
- **i.e.: WHEN DOES MY LOAN FUND?**
- **i.e.: WHY IS MY INTEREST RATE SO HIGH?**

Do not explain documents. You may provide limited answers. i.e.: Where is my APR? (Annual Percentage Rate) You can show them where the APR is located within the documents.

17. All loan documents are not created equal! As you are processing the loan document package, you may happen to notice that a particular document that you are use to seeing, is not there. Don't panic. It probably wasn't necessary for that particular type of loan. Remember, it's not your responsibility to make sure all documents are enclosed in the package. YOU did NOT create the loan.

18. As a notary public who is processing a loan document package remember…

    You are either to use the Acknowledgment or Jurat instruction on the loan document.

    The name of the document or type of document can be different in every case, including ones you are not familiar with. But the type of notary instructions on the document will only be an Acknowledgment or Jurat. That does not change. If you use a loose leaf certificate, the same will be true. Loose leaf certificates will either be an Acknowledgment or Jurat.

    You *really need* to understand this concept. It will make your notary process so much easier.

19. As a notary public who is processing a loan document package remember…

    If you see the phrase "WITNESS THE HAND(S) AND SEAL(S) OF THE UNDERSIGNED", or just the word "SEAL" - this does not mean the document needs to be notarized. You will notarize only if the document has actual notary language, or has an attached loose leaf certificate (Acknowledgment or Jurat) for notarization.

*THIS PAGE LEFT BLANK INTENTIONALLY*

## *AS A NOTARY PUBLIC LOAN SIGNING AGENT ABSOLUTELY NEVER...*

- **Absolutely Never** fail to be meticulous in all your Journal Entries! Our personal guideline: Make sure you could explain or defend any entry you have made in your Sequential Journal. Document everything that took place during that particular notary.

- **Absolutely Never** read a document! Scan it for completeness only. You must verify how every page impacts you as a notary public. You will review every page and determine if it has to be signed, initialed, or signed and notarized.

- **Absolutely Never** touch anything that belongs to the principal. You will ask the principal to remove their identification from their wallet. You can touch the documents. That is it! Don't set yourself up for a law suit. When the process is complete, hand the identification source back to the principal.

- **Absolutely Never** forget that you cannot use pencil to process your signings. Only blue or black ink!

- **Absolutely Never** mark or highlight the document to indicate where the borrower(s) need to sign or initial the document. Use "sign here" stickers or Post-it notes for reference.

- **Absolutely Never** forget to collect all of your supplies (especially your Commission Stamp, Embosser and Sequential Journal) after your notarization is complete...

- **Absolutely Never** forget to confirm the principles ID (Required by California State Code).

- **Absolutely Never** accept an expired ID.

- **Absolutely Never** notarize an incomplete document. Remember, documents that are *not* notarized within a loan package, can have blank spaces to be signed.

## *AS A NOTARY PUBLIC LOAN SIGNING AGENT ABSOLUTELY NEVER...*

*Continued*

- **Absolutely Never** give legal advice regarding any document in the loan document package.
- **Absolutely Never** change documents you are notarizing. (Unless it is within the notarial instructions).
- **Absolutely Never** backdate or postdate a document.
- **Absolutely Never** backdate or postdate your Sequential Journal.
- **Absolutely Never** use an interpreter...end of discussion.
- **Absolutely Never** rush through the loan signing process.

# BASIC MARKETING IDEAS FOR THE LOAN SIGNING AGENT AND MOBILE NOTARY PUBLIC

## FIRST THINGS FIRST...

**BUSINESS CARDS:**

- Have them made professionally
- If you elect to make them yourself, be sure they *look* professional!

**POTENTIAL LOAN SIGNING CLIENTS:**

- Signing Agents
- Title Companies
- Lenders
- Banks
- Savings & Loan Companies
- Real Estate Companies

**VISIT:**

- Hospitals
- Convalescent Homes
- Mobile Home Parks
- Assisted Living Housing Developments
- Senior Centers
- Attorney Offices
- Doctors Office
- Business Complexes

**CREATE YOUR LETTER OF INTRODUCTION:**

When visiting any of the above, present your business card and your letter of introduction for their reference. Depending upon the type of business you are visiting, you can ask for the person in charge of Administration, Office Manager, Human Resource Manager, Manager, or Owner.

**GIVE YOUR BUSINESS CARD TO ANYONE AND EVERYONE:**

You never know who you are giving it to...it could be the CEO of a large title company. Always give your business card to anyone you notarize for...let them know you travel, and you would be happy to assist them in the future!

**DRESS PROFESSIONALLY:**

Remember...you only have one opportunity to make a great first impression. Smile. Make eye contact when speaking to an individual. Be confident.

### *Following is a draft of a generic "Letter of Introduction" for your reference.*

Now That I'm a California Notary
Public... What the "*heck*" do I do? 8941
Atlanta Avenue #250 Huntington
Beach, CA 92646

**<u>RE: Mobile Notary Services and Loan Document Signing Services</u>**

This letter serves to introduce myself. My name is ____________ and I am a mobile Notary Public and Loan Document Signing Specialist. I am an experienced Notary Public. I have taken extensive courses for Notary and Loan Signing services. I am very energetic, and personable. I pride myself in paying attention to detail. If a challenge arises, I do everything possible to solve the issue.

I will always be diligent at representing your company with the highest regard for professionalism.

I am available (put your hours of availability and state any evening and weekend hours you will work).

My notary fees are based on the State of California Notary Fee Schedule. My travel fees are negotiable, depending upon the circumstances. In the case of a Loan Signing, my fee will be set at the time I receive your phone call. We will discuss all fees to be sure we agree to them, prior to the notarization service.

I will be happy to discuss your current needs at your convenience. I will call you within the next few days to follow up. I look forward to meeting with you to discuss how my experience and service could benefit you and your company. You may contact me at (phone number, pager, etc).

Thank you in advance for your time and consideration.
Sincerely,

Your name goes here.

# *"SAMPLE LETTER"*

***(Please feel free to use this format).***

***THIS PAGE LEFT BLANK INTENTIONALLY***

**ACKNOWLEDGMENT:** A Notarial Act in which the Notary certifies to have either personally known, or positively identified a principal who personally appeared before the Notary and admitted signing the document freely.

**AFFIANT:** A person who has accepted the oath or affirmation freely and signer of an affidavit.

**AFFIRMATION:** Solemn promise based on personal honor, without reference to God, made before a Notary for the completion of Notary service of a Jurat.

**AGENT:** A person authorized by another to act for or in place of him.

**ATTORNEY- IN-FACT:** A person, assigned through the completion of a power-of-attorney document, to act on behalf of another individual or principal to sign his or her name to specific documents.

**AUTHENTICATION:** By attachment of a Certificate of Authority, proving the genuineness of the signature, seal of the Notary or other official.

**BENEFICIARY:** One who holds equitable title to property being held in trust, such property being cared for by the trustee. [See fiduciary duty.]

**BOND:** Certificate which evidences a corporate debt. It is a security which involves no ownership interest in the issuing corporation.

**CERTIFIED COPY:** A document that verifies an original document as an accurate reproduction held by the custodian.

**CODICIL:** A written supplement or modification of a will. Codicils must be executed with the same formalities as a will.

**COMPENSATORY DAMAGES:** Money award equivalent to the actual value of injuries or damages sustained by the aggrieved party.

**COMPETENCE:** The ability to understand.

**CREDIBLE WITNESS:** An individual who is personally known to the Notary, or two individuals who by proper identification swears or affirms to the identity of another who is in the presence of, but is not personally known to the Notary.

**DAMAGES:** Money sought as a remedy for a breach of contract action or for tortuous acts.

**DECEIT:** A false representation of facts made recklessly, maliciously, or with knowledge of its falsity, with the intent to cause the injured person to rely on the misrepresentation.

**DEED:** A document by which title to property [usually real property] is passed.

**DEPOSE:** To make a deposition; to testify under oath or affirmation verbally or in writing.

**EMPLOYEE:** A person who works for an employer for salary or wages.

**ESTATE:** Extent of ownership or interest one has in property.

**FELONY:** Crime which carries the most severe sanctions, usually ranging form one year in a state or federal prison to the forfeiture of one's life.

**FIDUCIARY DUTY:** A duty to act for someone else's benefit, while subordinating one's personal interests to that of the other person. It is the highest standard of duty implied by law.

**FORGERY:** A false signature, writing, document or personal identification or other device created or made to imitate a genuine signature, writing, document or other official creation; the act of making a false document, with the intent to defraud.

**FRAUD:** An act, through the use of deception, that is aimed at causing a person unknowingly to surrender an item of value, right to, or advantages without proper compensation; Any misrepresentation either by misstatement or omission of a material fact knowingly made with the intention of misrepresentation to another and on which a reasonable person would and does rely to his or her detriment.

**GRANTOR:** A person who transfers property or creates a trust.

**HOLDER:** A person who is in possession of a document.

**HOLOGRAPHIC DOCUMENT:** A Will or Deed written entirely in the signer's handwriting, usually not witnessed.

**IDENTIFICATION:** Proof that a person is who he purported or represented himself to be.

**IMPARTIAL WITNESS:** An Unbiased observer, a Commissioned Notary Public.

**IMPLIED AUTHORITY:** The power of an agent to act on behalf of his principal who is inferred to from the Responsibilities imposed on the agent or necessary to carry out an agent's express authority.

**INCIDENTAL BENEFICIARY**: A person who indirectly receives, or will receive, a benefit as the result of a Contract entered into other parties. The incidental beneficiary is neither a donor beneficiary nor a creditor beneficiary and thus has no right to enforce the contract.

**INNOCENT MISREPRESENTATION**: A false statement of fact or act made in good faith which deceives and causes harm or injury to another.

**INSTRUMENT**: A formal or legal document in writing.

**JURAT**: Notarial act in which a Commissioned Notary Public gives or administers an oath or affirmation and Witnesses the signing of the document which is declared by the signer to be true and correct.

**LIABILITY**: Being responsible for one's lawful actions or being held responsible for any acts of misconduct or omissions.

**MISCONDUCT**: The performance of a prohibited action or actions, or failing to perform a lawful or required action.

**MISDEMEANOR**: Lessor crime, punishable by fine or punishment other than a state or federal penitentiary, as opposed to a felony.

**NEGLIGENCE**: Conduct which falls below the standard of care which would be exercised by the "reasonable person," in relation to the protection of others. A legal duty is inherent in negligence.

**NOTARIAL CERTIFICATE**: A document or attached document describing the particulars of the original document which requires the insertion of the Commissioned Notary Public signature and seal affixed.

**OATH**: A solemn promise to God made before a Ministerial official involving in a relation to a Jurat or as a notarial act in its own rights.

**PERJURY**: Crime of making a false statement under oath or affirmation in any official proceedings.

**PERSONAL KNOWLEDGE**: Familiarity with an individual resulting from personal interactions over a given period of time sufficient to eliminate reasonable doubt that the individual is the person claimed.

*GLOSSARY OF NOTARY TERMS*

**POSITIVE IDENTIFICATION**: By the use of acceptable credible identification as evidence to prove an individual is that person he claims to be.

**POWER OF ATTORNEY**: A document or instrument authorizing another to act as one's agent or attorney.

**PRINCIPLE**: In agency, a person who, by agreement or otherwise, authorizes an agent to act on his or her behalf such that the acts of the agent become binding on the principle.

**PROBABLE CAUSE**: Reasonable ground to believe the existence of facts warranting certain actions such as the search or arrest of a person.

**PROTEST**: Archaic notarial act in which a Notary certifies that a constituent did not receive payment.

**PUNITIVE DAMAGES**: Compensation in excess of actual or consequential damages. They are awarded in order to punish the wrongdoer, and will be awarded only in cases involving willful or malicious misconduct.

**QUIT CLAIM DEED**: A deed conveying whatever title or interest the grantor has in the real property, but warrants nothing, not even the transferor's title, to the grantee.

**REASONABLE CARE**: Degree of attentiveness and precaution expected of a person of ordinary prudence and intelligence.

**REASONABLE DOUBT:** The standard used to determine the guilt or innocence of a person criminally charged. To be guilty of a crime, one must be proved guilty "beyond and to the exclusion of every reasonable doubt." A doubt that would cause prudent persons to hesitate before acting in matters important to themselves.

**REVOCATION**: The recall of the Notary Public commission, authority given, or thing granted, or a destroying or making void of some will, deed, or offer that has been valid till revoked.

**SIGNATURE**: the name or mark of a person, written by himself, or at his direction. In commercial law, any name, word, or mark used with the intention to notarize writing -constitutes a signature.

**SUBSCRIBING WITNESS:** A person who is personally known to the Notary or proven on the oath or affirmation of a Credible Witness who is personally known to the Notary, to be the person whose name is subscribed to a document or instrument, who, is duly sworn and deposes and says he/she was present and saw that same person described in the document or instrument sign the document.

**TESTATOR/TESTATRIX**- [male/female] A person who makes and executes a will.

**TITLE**: The formal right of ownership of property.

**TRUSTEE**: One who holds legal title to property "in trust" for the benefit of another person [beneficiary], and who must carry out specific duties with regard to the property. The trustee owes a fiduciary duty to the beneficiary.

**UNDUE INFLUENCE**: Abuse of one's position of influence or relationship with another person by overcoming that person's free will, persuading that person to act or refrain from acting in a certain manner.

**VALID CONTRACT**: A properly constituted contract having legal strength or force.

**VENUE**: The location (state or county) where a Notary service is performed, as indicated at the top of all notarial certificates.

**WILL**: An instrument directing what is to be done with a person's property upon his or her death, made by that person and revocable during lifetime.

## *NOTES*

## *NOTES*

# *NOTES*

# *NOTES*

AUTHORS eMail address

slh92646@yahoo.com

SECRETARY OF STATE 916.653.3595

4124774R00061

Made in the USA
San Bernardino, CA
05 September 2013